"Recovered Memory" and Other Assaults
Upon the Mysteries of Consciousness

"Recovered Memory" and Other Assaults Upon the Mysteries of Consciousness

Hypnosis, Psychotherapy, Fraud and the Mass Media

by
WILLIAM ROGERS

McFarland & Company, Inc., Publishers
Jefferson, North Carolina, and London

British Library Cataloguing-in-Publication data are available

Library of Congress Cataloguing-in-Publication Data

Rogers, William, 1944–
    Recovered memory and other assaults upon the mysteries of
consciousness : hypnosis, psychotherapy, fraud and the mass media /
by William Rogers.
        p.   cm.
    Includes bibliographical references and index.
    ISBN 0-7864-0109-5 (lib. bdg. : 55# alk. paper) ∞
    1. Consciousness.   2. Altered states of consciousness.
3. Recollection (Psychology)   4. False memory syndrome.
5. Psychotherapy.   I. Title.
BF311.R62   1995
150—dc20   95-15794
                                                                CIP

Manufactured in the United States of America

McFarland & Company, Inc., Publishers
    Box 611, Jefferson, North Carolina 28640

In memory of
Sunny J. Rogers

Table of Contents

Introduction

The purpose of this work is to help the reader understand how consciousness is related to pragmatic human processes within the context of socialization. Consciousness is one of the most profound and puzzling facets of the human condition. It is not clearly known what it is or even *how* it is. Since the nature of the topic does not lend itself well to standard inquiry, the question of how to study consciousness in the first place becomes a major challenge.

This book begins with an examination of methods of inquiry, a determination as to which of them can and cannot be useful, with the rationale for such conclusions; hermeneutics is chosen as the inquiry method of choice. There follows a thorough investigation into the multiplicities of consciousness. Finally, there is an in-depth investigation of the manipulation and influence of environmental issues on human consciousness.

Implications are that different negative (erroneous and harmful) and positive (correct and useful) altered states of reality at both social and individual levels can result in and from influences on consciousness. There is strong indication of dissemination of misleading information in a number of significant areas, including hypnosis, retrowareness, counseling psychology, recovered memory, contemporary parenting procedures, and factors concerning racial societal mainstreaming. Much of this destructive information is either initiated or accepted and aggrandized by the mass media. The overall impact of such pervasive erroneous information has resulted in dysfunctional consequences throughout the human cycle of development, one major result being the inability of a large number of persons to take responsibility for their own lives.

To reach these conclusions, one must first confront this question, which exists in a multiplicity and variation of forms: What is consciousness? Is consciousness at all tangible? Is it something which has physicality? Does consciousness exist on an individual level or only on a social plane? Is consciousness even an entity that can actually be termed "real"? Finally, what constitutes a good, clear, precise definition of consciousness?

As one might expect, there is no general consensus about what the "true" explanation of consciousness should be. For example, some scientists believe consciousness to be a homeostatic regulating system which exists in all living organisms which possess a brain (Masden, 1984). Others see "mind" as a part of the brain and consciousness as only a part of "mind," which has a partial separation from brain. In this view, consciousness exists only in higher brains, belonging only to the human animal (Crick and Koch, 1992).

The definition and study of consciousness, to be effective, must first orient the theorist to the investigation of beginnings: the biological foundation for living things, the history of consciousness, past studies and methodological orientations, leading to current trends in research and contemporary status. Finally, there needs to be a pragmatic look at utilitarian implications for such fields as education, health services, and psychotherapy (Lycan, 1987).

As we go back in time so that we might try to understand the "birth" of what *is*, we must have some concept of why anyone should be interested in undertaking or reading about such a massive quest to "know" the unknowable. Why is it important enough to dedicate the time needed for proper research? How will the results of such inquiry be beneficial to humankind?

Many of the answers as to why it would be important and useful for us to understand the initial formulation, the current coagulated ingredients, and the future potential of consciousness are blatantly obvious. To know consciousness is to understand thought, to understand the "mind-body problem," to comprehend the most integral part of the recipe of what it means to be human. And, as we scientifically travel the investigative path from the very beginnings to today, other reasons arise.

Within the scientific arena of neurobiology, consciousness is generally defined as awareness, that is to say, being aware of one's existence in a subjective and finite fashion. It is also, of course, much more than that. Thomas Natsoulas (1978, 1983) places the differing states of consciousness under seven primary headings: joint or mutual knowledge, internal knowledge or conviction, awareness, direct awareness, personal unity, the normal waking state, and double consciousness. A similar but not identical point of view is that consciousness is basically a fundamental fact of human existence which relates to the direct, subjective nature of people's awareness of their own experiences. One can, in fact, only be aware of one's own consciousness; it is impossible to be aware, first-hand, of someone else's consciousness (Farthing, 1992).

The solution to the problem of understanding consciousness has to come through a closer collaboration among neuroscientists, theorists, and humanistic psychologists. There will also have to be a shifting of methods of inquiry from the natural science arena toward procedures more suited to the study of living, breathing, behaving humans, such as existential-phenomenological and hermeneutic systems (Polkinghorne, 1983). A large number of interacting difficulties among the varying branches of research will need to be overcome. However, consciousness is now considered by many to be the most profound and puzzling facet of the human condition ("Mind and Brain," 1992). Therefore, to be a small part of the investigatory siege could turn out to be the exhilarating ride of the ages.

The purpose of this study is to begin to see how consciousness is related to other processes, for example, the socialization process and the cultural context. From that basic foundation we will begin to understand more clearly the meaning or meanings of consciousness itself. The primary research question is: *What are the various contexts from which the interpretation of consciousness arises in relation to its impact on different realities (altered states)?*

An altered state of consciousness is defined in almost as many ways as there are scientists studying the subject. Probably the main reason for this is because "altered states" is a theoretical construct— as is the term "consciousness," for that matter. For our purposes, altered states of consciousness (ASCs) are basically abstract cognitive phenomena which exteriorize human perceptive and social processes. In other words, an ASC would be any major change of understanding or point of view from the norm: what one believed before, one does not believe now; what was the norm is now a different norm.

This book explores the sociocultural context, the semantic context, and the "lived body" context of certain specific ASCs. It is an attempt to understand a network of experiences that are all related to that which is consciousness. From there we will expand to different possible states of awareness, or what can also be called "reality." We begin with the foundational question of methods of inquiry: the primary puzzle has always been how to *study* consciousness. Then we turn to the major topics which have proven to be erroneous and harmful, such as "recovered memory," some forms of psychotherapy, hypnosis, "retrowareness," autistic facilitation, and much of the "pop" methodology of contemporary child rearing. By formulating and defining more specifically both the positive and negative potential consequences of these different "realities" we can generate a better psychological understanding of the inner and outer experiences and behaviors of the human condition, which, in a potentially astonishing way, could be quite helpful throughout the mental health field.

The methodology of this inquiry is based on the utilization of hermeneutics, which is an approach that emphasizes meanings from a multiplicity of differing viewpoints and for which language is an integral part of understanding. For example, any single word or symbol cannot help but refer to many overlapping meanings. Therefore, in order to begin to investigate and comprehend consciousness at all, one must first determine and define the several different foundational concepts of the term and conclude which ones are most compatible with both known scientific data and continued ongoing scrutiny (Aron, 1982; Polkinghorne, 1983).

Our inquiry begins with an examination of the term "consciousness" specifically as it relates to understanding pertaining to language. There is really no other logical way to communicate such a concept. Then follows an investigation concerning different definitions from separate viewpoints and from within different contexts. This relates to books, articles, papers, and a great deal of other literature on the subject, as well as third-person experience and personal experience. From this modality we derive what is called "multi-dimensional significance" that is able to describe consciousness in behavioral, cognitive, physiological, and experiential terms (Barrell, 1985). There is also a stage or process of investigation called *differentiation*, which delves into the representations of similarities and oppositions, that is, those terms, symbols, words, and experiences which are sometimes like consciousness and sometimes confused with consciousness but are *not* consciousness.

Hermeneutics recognizes that a human phenomenon is basically an expression of meaning and, therefore, can best be understood from multiple frames of reference and by means of multiple frames of inquiry. It is an approach that offers a methodology for more fully comprehending the nature of a given phenomenon. It allows new understandings to arise, which themselves create new questions and a continuation of the procedure. This process is referred to as "the hermeneutic circle," a continually emerging formulation of information and interpretation that results in an ever-broadening understanding of consciousness. This process does not attempt to end or conclude somewhere; it simply continues to broaden and deepen one's understanding of the topic being explored. However, from this expanded understanding come new generalizations and insights about consciousness, and from there one can bring forth specific recommendations which may be helpful in the field of psychology as well as many other areas of pragmatic utilization.

CHAPTER 1

Methods of Inquiry

Pseudoscience

The purpose of this scientific investigation is to gain useful data on consciousness. To do so, one must apply scientific methods, not pseudoscientific methods, and all the while must never underestimate the national appetite for bogus revelation. This comment is a paraphrase of a response by H. L. Mencken (1917) to the famous circus sideshows of one P. T. Barnum, the most successful entertainer of his day. If anything, belief in the bizarre has a larger audience now than ever before. No one knows exactly why this is, but it may have to do with not wanting to take responsibility for one's own life.

"Pseudo" comes from the Greek word *pseudes*, which means "to deceive." Other derivatives of the meaning are false, sham, pretended, and fictitious. In other words, pseudoscience is not a science at all. It is deceptive, spurious, and counterfeit. The conclusions of pseudoscience have very little, if any, basis in known fact. The results are simply formulated to fit a particular story. Pseudoscience is characterized by anachronistic thinking, by appeals to myths, by a refusal to revise in light of legitimate criticism, and by recourse to irrefutable hypotheses (Radner and Radner, 1982). An anachronism is something that is in the wrong time frame. It may have "fit" at one time, but it does not now. Believing the earth to be flat, for example, may have been legitimate thinking 800 years ago, but it would be quite unreasonable today. Many pseudoscientific "revelations" appeal to myths. Stories about spaceships, Martians, and time travel all have mythological foundations. Using a biblical story thousands of years old or even an ancient fairy tale as the basis for "truth" is a mainstay tool of the spinners of contemporary pseudoscientific mysteries.

The core of any truly scientific hypothesis is that it must be refutable (Radner and Radner, 1982). This does not necessarily mean that it ever will be disproved or negated, but that possibility has to at least exist. If there is nothing that would constitute good evidence against a particular hypothesis, then that hypothesis cannot be claimed as scientific. For example, if objects did not fall to the ground when dropped (a change of fact) then the theory of gravity could be refuted. But the fact that bones can be carbon-dated and shown to be tens of thousands of years old does not affect the hypothesis of creationism. Since "God can do all things," he can easily make bones look very old when, in fact, they are not. End of argument.

Another method of pseudoscience has to do with "fact" gathering. One simply has to state a "fact" and it will stand on its own. There is no need to actually explain it. A famous example occurred in London in 1661, when the Royal Society announced in its publication that one of its members had promised to bring a unicorn's horn to the next meeting. In the publication a month later, it was noted that a demonstration had been performed with the powder of a unicorn's horn. Hence, the unicorn horn was a "fact." Just saying it somehow made it so (Radner and Radner, 1982).

Scientific methodology is of a different leaning altogether. Wanting to know the answer to something, of course, begins with a question. Everywhere we look, we observe things that cause us to speculate, to wonder, to ask questions. This is the start, the beginning, of the road that leads to the process of research. Research is where the paths of the methodologies of science and pseudoscience sharply divide.

Scientific research requires, first of all, a clear understanding of what it is that needs to be done and the precise articulation of a goal. What is the problem to be solved? If the scientist does not have a total comprehension of what is intended, without vagueness, then the very foundation of the premise has cracks in it and will fall to pieces before the task is completed.

Science is usually defined as systematized knowledge derived from observation, study, and experimentation carried out in order to determine the nature or principles of what is being studied. The scientific method offers systematic description, explanation, prediction, and control. Research is a "search" for a reliable demonstration of the workings of some part of the actual world (Goldstein and

Goldstein, 1978). This discernment is brought about, ideally, by following general laws and principles that can be examined by experimental testing. Even valid scientific structuring has much differentiation within its legitimate boundaries. There are three basic subcategories of scientific methodology: historical, experimental, and observational (Siever, 1968). These categories are relevant to the ongoing argument about whether there is only one science or several sciences. These three research "explanations" are of the utmost importance to a topic as difficult to grasp as consciousness.

Experimental science is mostly associated with analytical processes. "Analysis" means the separating or breaking up of any whole into its parts to find out its nature. Observational science is totally descriptive; it involves watching, noting, and recording facts and events for later comments and conclusions. Historical science has no important differences from non-historical science (Siever, 1968). For example, it does not matter specifically how the Grand Canyon was formed in terms of chronological time and geological processes. It matters only how large canyons, in general, were formed. There would be an exception, of course, in the case of something that only happened once.

Pseudoscience can be fun, interesting, and entertaining. With a good marketing strategy, a lot of money can be made from it. Pseudoscience can also be educational, insofar as it demonstrates how *not* to conduct science, or what science is not (Radner and Radner, 1982). However, valid science can be even more interesting, fun, and exciting. The topics being investigated are even more astonishing than those of pseudoscience, and it is *real*, not make believe. Therein lies all the difference in the world.

Mainstream Research

Let us now take a critical view of "standard" methods of inquiry. What is the "right" way to conduct scientific investigations? What is proper, what is allowed, and what is not allowed? These questions are coming to the fore quite frequently in contemporary philosophic circles, especially in the study of the "human condition." In this section we will take a clear look at the major features of what is considered by most to be the standard method of operation of the "legitimate" scientific world. We will discover what has consensus merit within the multiplicity of procedures and what may not, in fact, have as much merit as had been previously believed.

The dominant overall position pertaining to the gathering of information for the purpose of scientific endeavor relates most specifically to how one studies the natural sciences. The current method of thinking has its basis in two paramount claims: that the path of scientific righteousness is paved with investigation through *empirical* means, and that this information is best understood through the use of empiricist and positivist guidelines. Basically, empiricists argue that legitimate knowledge must be founded primarily on input from the senses, that is, as opposed to being intuitive. Positivism, simply put, requires that scientists come up with conclusions that they are totally sure about; educated guesswork or speculation is not scientific. The actuality of the information, then, is something about which the scientist must be positive.

Inquiry into the community of contemporary scientists indicates that the profession may be split into two important parts, empirical and nonempirical. Through empirical methods, scientists attempt to investigate events by explanation, description, and exploration. The data that are retrieved in this manner must stand up to scrutiny with what we know to be experiential facts (Hempel, 1966). Final acceptance depends on whether or not the concluding statements can be supported by such methods as systematic observation, clinical evaluation, and experimentation.

The empirical approach rests on the belief that direct observation and experience provide the only firm basis for understanding natural events (Hempel, 1966). Questions asked under the preceding guidelines are referred to as "empirical questions," that is, any questions that can be answered by objective observation. For example, Does a deprived early environment result in low intelligence? Is capital punishment an effective deterrent to murder? These potential variables can be defined in terms of observable characteristics.

Generally speaking, standard acceptable scientific knowledge is arrived at by developing a hypothesis (testable predictions derived from theory) as the possible answer to a particular problem or question and then subjecting the possibilities to empirical testing (Hempel, 1966). The systematic study of human behavior begins with theories, that is, general explanations or statements that may or may not be proved correct through research. In order to be tested, a theory must be broken down into more limited statements — hypotheses.

Nonexperimental studies are simply those in which information is not gathered by experimentation. The data accumulated describe some aspect of naturally occurring behavior and the information collected may result in a theory or hypothesis to explain the observation. The researchers have no direct control over the independent variable. Instead, they must simply record the effects of an observable operation as it occurs in a real-life situation (Penrod, 1986).

One of the main reasons for the questioning of the "standard view" of scientific research is concerns over its application to human study (Polkinghorne, 1983). There seems to be a growing belief that the human dimension adds a number of new elements to the puzzle which call for different methods of investigation. At the very root of this is the fact that animate inquiry differs from inanimate inquiry. This fact alone makes the question relevant to consciousness studies.

Let us take a closer look at the positivist model, as described by Donald Polkinghorne (1983). There are human characteristics and processes that constitute a form of reality in that they occur under a wide variety of conditions and thus can be generalized to some degree. A complex process may be studied independently when related to different variables. For example, attempting to understand the effects of teacher behavior on student learning can be adequately investigated without studying all of the possible factors that influence student learning. Such inquiry can gradually merge into a composite picture of the phenomenon being investigated. Finally, when enough investigation has been carried out, one can control and predict the phenomenon at levels that greatly exceed chance. The researcher can also function independently from the subject to a major degree. The ultimate goal of the research is to develop a body of knowledge in the form of generalizations that will hold, at least to some degree, in contexts similar to those in which the generalizations were developed. Developing general and all-embracing theories is the paramount purpose of science, according to the positivist point of view. Events can be understood and described through the correlation of test results conducted in accordance with empirical methods.

However useful this approach, by the middle of the twentieth century adherents of this view had failed to show with certainty that its resulting statements and conclusions could be backed up by experience through the senses. The empirical data of positivist investigation were not being accepted and formulated as consensus "truth," as far as the stated empirical laws were concerned. So began much of the criticism.

Many contemporary critics of the orthodox view of science believe it is supported by several faulty tenets. They maintain that there are important questions about the so-called absolute distinction between theoretical terms and direct observation, that time sequences must be accounted for in connection with experimental correlations when linking theory to goings-on in the world at large, and that theories should not be looked at as truisms or maxims (Polkinghorne, 1983).

Basically, these critics say that the use of inductive (specific to general) and deductive (general to specific) reasoning to formulate theories does not provide a large enough template for adequate studies of the human condition. Polkinghorne offers another discipline, historical realism, as better suited to achieving a more complete integration of methodologies, including the "standard view," along with a more human-oriented repertoire taking into consideration the varied phenomena of humankind. A human is not a rock or a tree or a beetle. Even though we are made from the same cosmic "stuff," we have evolved further up the evolutionary ladder. Consequently, we have certain attributes which other things do not. These attributes may need to be investigated by different methodologies.

This ongoing debate about the variances between the right and wrong of natural sciences and human sciences began to take shape in the latter part of the nineteenth century. This was a period when the dominant physical sciences were ruled by what were believed to be natural laws of the universe. These natural laws were based on what was tangible, measurable, and specific—atoms, molecules, protons, neutrons, and such (Polkinghorne, 1983). In what seemed an obvious analog, an attempt was made to apply the same measuring stick to human behavior. Those who believed that it was misdirected to apply natural science methodology to the study of humanity put forth a demand for the creation of a "new science."

For the sciences dealing with human behavior to become more

workable as a means to true understanding, it is believed by the critics of the "standard view" that a comprehension of the *meaning* of being human must be brought to the fore. That is to say, the nuance of "humanness" is integral to making sense of the study of the species. Consequently, they conclude that the current dominant scientific view is far too limited by its empiricist principles to allow the "politics" of being human to be brought into consideration, which leaves out much of what interactive, social human reality is actually about. Thus, a "new science" has to be formulated and made ready for full acceptance within the mainstream scientific community (Taylor, [1971] 1977).

Another interesting criticism of the "standard view" of science has to do with the belief that somehow this approach is the one most untouched by subjectivity. The scientist is seen as coming to totally objective conclusions based on a completely unprejudiced understanding of the "facts" before him or her. As Kuhn (1963) points out, this view, of course, is mythical. All humans bring very personal points of view into their everyday interactions; scientists are no different. Researchers will often achieve the results and come to the conclusions they were looking for and expecting; without the researcher being consciously aware of it, the "facts" are made to conform with the desired answers. Though stated in a positive and arrogant manner, they may turn out, after all, to be educated opinions, repeated over and over again and widely believed, when they are nothing more than dogma and often far removed from the truth (Kuhn, 1963).

A close look at another element in the contemporary reign of epistemological methodology in psychological research exposes a bias concerning what are called the "self-processes." Some of the tenets of the concept of self-processes are that people have a tendency to put forth an enhanced positive self-image in order to boost self-esteem, that the nature of the self-process is humanly interactive, and that it has a definite impact on all psychological research (Hales, 1986). Consequently, in research with human subject, manipulation of the self-image will absolutely come into play. This need or desire to gloss over these dynamics in a laboratory situation can pertain both to those being investigated and to those doing the investigating. Research methods that accord with the "standard view" are quite adept at providing answers to certain types of questions. However, when the human equation comes into consideration, a "new science" is needed, one that accepts the need for a human-factored, integrated methodology (Polkinghorne, 1983; Hales, 1986).

Taken together, all of the criticisms of the "standard view" of science touched upon in this section can be seen to mesh into one encompassing argument. The scientific method does serve well in understanding natural phenomena. However, the "standard view" does not suffice when considering unique human beings or their potential for growth or regression. The living subject is not and cannot be static; therefore, the time has come for a separate and equally valid "human science" methodology. This methodology includes hermeneutics, a discipline which is employed throughout this work.

Is the understanding of human consciousness, on anything other than the personal level, possible at all? We can certainly offer any number of reasons, causes, and meanings pertaining to human expression. However, any such explanation can only be the viewer's *perception* of an observed behavior. It is not the viewed person's reality, but the viewer's. Therefore, we must certainly research those "realities."

There is a view that states that to make meaningful progress in the area of consciousness studies we have to change from an "observed system reality" (the notion that we can know the objective truth about others and ourselves) to an "observing system reality" (the notion that we can know only our own construction of others, as well as of ourselves). The meaning of what I am doing (thinking) at any given time can be comprehended, if at all, only by me, and, "conscious-wise," maybe not even me. The basic structure of the human nervous system dictates such a conclusion (Hoffman, 1988).

In order to research and discuss consciousness, one must be conscious, and one must be aware of being conscious. But then there is the problem of what being "aware" means. The only individual one can be personally aware of is oneself. The "self-referential position" is at the core of the problems connected with formulating an acceptable methodology. This leads to the argument put forth by a certain segment of the scientific community that there needs to be a shift in paradigm, to take into account the "self-knowing" element of experiential knowledge (Miller, 1992). However, one has to take care not to accept data that heretofore did not "make sense," that is, were not rational.

What is "rational"? The concept of relativism has to come into play when one begins to ask any number of questions pertaining to standards of rationality. Some persons prefer ice cream to candy; some prefer candy to ice cream. This is simply a difference in taste. Some persons think it wrong to kill other creatures for the purpose of eating them; some do not. Is this a matter of taste? What makes an action right? What makes a person praiseworthy? Again, what is "rational"? It may very well be that the rationality of an action, an answer, a behavior, a conclusion, or anything else might have relevance only to its own cultural construction (Polkinghorne, 1983).

One of the important methodological issues relating to the study of consciousness has to do with the "mind-body question." That is, what is the connection between the body (brain) and the mind (consciousness)? While opinion ranges across a broad spectrum, the arguments fall into two general categories. According to one view, associated with the philosophical position known as dualism, the brain and the mind are different entities: whereas the brain is tangible, the mind is more ethereal, on the periphery of what is actually measurable. On the other side is the view that the body and the mind are inextricably intertwined. This position, known as materialism, holds that brain events are the cause of mental events (Farthing, 1992).

A major problem surrounding the study of consciousness is mistaking or not understanding causal relationships in behavior. What the observer *perceived* is not what the one being observed may have *meant* (Miller, 1992). For example, correspondent inferences can be made from "noncommon" behavior: A man rolls up his sleeve and scratches his arm. You determine that his arm itches; but the man's rolling up his sleeve is not necessarily a common event, so you could not have legitimately come to that conclusion simply from that one act. This illustrates how easy it is to misunderstand the meaning of behavior even at the most overt level. If that is so, the understanding of another person's "inner experience" would seem an even more formidable task.

In order to formulate a more successful method of studying and understanding consciousness, the "rules of the game" — the ways of thinking about the conceivability of measuring and comprehending self-awareness — are being altered. The evolution of ideas about the physics of thinking, which can be traced from Aristotle to Einstein, is now taking a further step (Watkins and Watkins, 1986).

As the methodology of research pertaining to consciousness is still being worked out, one continues to have to address a number of basic issues which are somewhat different from "normal" research issues. One of these ingredients relates to determining what *really* exists and what does not exist. In philosophy, this is what is called an ontological problem. What are mental states, exactly where do they take place, and how is the physical world connected to these processes? These fundamental questions relate to the original mind-body problem and the conflict between the dualist theory of the mind as essentially nonphysical in nature, with no direct connection to the brain, and the materialist theory, which states that the mind is merely part of the complex physical system of the brain.

Another important stumbling block to consciousness research pertains to semantics (Churchland, 1983). Terms relating to any interactive endeavor are always somewhat dubious in their specificity. To define meaning in the realm of describing and knowing mental states is even more precarious. Even in its most overt form, when standard communication is taking place between persons, there are always at least two forms of language working at the same time: a conscious form of language and an unintentional, unconscious form of communication. Studies indicate that the conscious form of language emanates from the left brain and the unconscious form from the right brain (Wonder and Donovan, 1984). Besides the spoken word, such things as body movements, phrasing, emphasis, sighs, and tone of voice all send certain kinds of messages. On top of this, the messages themselves may be contradictory. Consequently, the ability to understand specific and valid meanings from "normal" human interactions is itself a task of some magnitude. Reaching a collective scientific agreement about the primary terminology necessary for optimal understanding of the mind-body problem may seem to be a task strewn with insurmountable roadblocks. Nevertheless, a way can be found, thanks to the fact that what is scientifically acceptable does not exclusively depend on what is certain. Acceptable data can simply be what has held up against standard tests of experiment and experience—the *best available* answer, term, meaning, or explanation (Polkinghorne, 1983).

In putting together a valid methodology for consciousness studies, another major frustration, alluded to earlier, is what is sometimes referred to as the "other mind problem." How can one person know anything at all about the "mental states" of another person?

Again, we come back to the problem of *my* perception of someone else's behavior. Otherwise, one would have to assume that another person's overt expression of his or her mental states is brought about by exactly the same "inner experience" as the observer's. Since it seems to be completely impossible that one individual could ever have direct experience of another individual's consciousness, this problem appears to be impossible to solve (Farthing, 1992). The question remains, How does one go about formulating valid research methods for the "science of the mind"? Does one stick totally to the tried-and-true empirical approach, or should one go over completely to the other side and claim a separate and distinct autonomy for research into mental states? Perhaps some combination of the two approaches is in order. What sort of epistemological information (that pertaining to knowledge and where it comes from) should be allowed as valid in this new kind of research? Finally, how can scientists formulate a consensus on these questions? The *science of interpretation*, hermeneutics, is one workable pathway.

Cognitive and Behavioral Paradigms

As stated earlier, the study of consciousness has become possibly the primary area of interest and investigation in psychology today. It is believed that researchers are finally moving toward some definitive conclusions concerning certain aspects of how and why consciousness exists and works (Scientific American, 1992). There is a multiplicity of types of consciousness, and several different paradigmatic ways of studying consciousness. There are also differences of opinion as to what questions are important and need answering and which do not. In this section I will compare and contrast the research paradigms of behavioral psychology and the branch of cognitive psychology known as social learning theory. In the next section we will look at the differences between experimental and observational methodologies. In this discussion, I use the term "consciousness" in the all-encompassing sense of general self-awareness, ignoring the multitude of sub-forms, such as internal knowledge or conviction, personal unity, or double consciousness (Natsoulas, 1978).

Before comparing the methodological paradigms of these two separate and specialized fields of psychology, let us clarify what a

paradigm is. Fundamentally, a paradigm is a set of assumptions de-
limiting an area to be investigated scientifically and specifying the
methods to be used to collect and interpret the resulting data. Put
another way, a paradigm is a general view used by scientists to direct
research (Borg and Gall, 1989). It defines the important questions to
be addressed and prescribes the acceptable methods of research. A
paradigm is the premise which dictates the models of investigation
and what is to be investigated. It is also important to understand the
concept of a paradigm shift. That structural movement takes place
when existing paradigms fail to provide adequate explanations for
new findings and a new paradigm emerges that helps to explain
original findings as well as new ones.

Another preliminary task is to clarify the differing philosophic
viewpoints of behavioral psychology and social learning theory. Behaviorists believe basically that human behavior differs from animal
behavior only in the degree of its complexity. Natural selection
shaped the human species to adapt to increasingly complex environ-
ments; but behavior is behavior, no matter what the organism (Watson, 1967). Thus, studying the "simpler" behavior of animals holds
the tantalizing promise of shedding light on the more complex behavior of humans. The basic tenet of behaviorism is that animal
(including human) behavior is related to cause-and-effect types of
conditioning; introspection is not a part of the ingredients. Behaviorism, it should be noted, does not deny the existence of mental states,
but disputes their importance in governing the actions (behavior) of
animals, including humans (Skinner, 1983).

There is much evidence, gathered in psychology studies over
the years, which shows that what a human being thinks, expects, and
plans for can directly regulate his or her behavior. What a person
deliberately plans, for example, has to be given as much weight as
his or her actual performance (Allport, 1961). This relates to the
foundational philosophy of social learning theory which states that
humans actively perceive and interpret stimuli in their environment
and use them to create meaning within their social interactions.
Thus, the scope of possible paradigms extends from the radical behaviorist view, that thinking is a *consequence* of behavior, to simple
cognitive behaviorism, which states thinking is a *cause* of behavior,
all the way to cognitive social learning, which puts forth the viewpoint that thinking can be a cause, a consequence, or a correlate of
behavior (Farber, 1963).

In comparing the different means of studying consciousness employed by behavioral psychology and cognitive social learning theory, one must retain a broad focus on the general meaning of consciousness. Examples of the problems connected with trying to cover too many types of consciousness are well shown by Baruss (1986-87) and Natsoulas (1978). The lines of specificity become skewed. This leads to difficulties in delineating the topic, which in turn lead to a considerable decrease in the understanding of consciousness necessary to follow the process.

Let us start by looking at how behavioral psychologists would investigate the given definition of consciousness. The behaviorist point of view (paradigm) identifies biology as the prime cause of human action. At the beginning of life it is the sole cause; as the child gets older, social stimuli begin to have an important, but still limited, controlling effect (Pattison and Kahan, 1986).

It is basic that the methodology of behaviorism does not lean toward the study of "unobservable" variables. Rather, it relates to actions taking place as the result of stimuli, either given or received, as in operant (behavior and consequences) or classical (stimulus response) conditioning. B. F. Skinner (1973) developed a reinforcement theory of action that did not rely on "inner" mechanisms. The concept is simply that thinking takes place only as a result of action. Consequently, a behaviorist study of consciousness would give no time and attach no importance to personal introspection. It would investigate only general awareness as it relates to external stimuli. The great strength of behaviorism is its method, which places great emphasis on observable, verifiable, and controllable variables, thus transforming psychology into experimental science.

According to behaviorists, the assumption that behavior is influenced by inner mental forces is unobservable and therefore undetectable and not testable. That being the case, consciousness studies would need to rely on those responses which were tangible and observable. The researcher, for example, could perform a cohort-sequential (similar age groups) design program which would include a group of subjects participating in cross-sectional (various ages at a specific point in time) and longitudinal (individuals at different points in time) components. This would allow the continuous tracking of these groups to determine the correctness of prediction and control of human behavior by examining stimulus-response relationships (Watson, 1967).

A key tool of behaviorist investigation is experimental methodology; introspection and subjective data are considered suspect. An example of this attitude is the view that dysfunctional symptoms are not signs of unconscious or even conscious conflicts. Such symptoms are just observable manifestations caused by errant conditioning and are changeable by new conditioning. Stated in another way, both normal and abnormal behavior are learned, and necessary and sufficient conditions of learning are found in principles of conditioning (Skinner, 1967). Consequently, one can study general consciousness only in a manner that would investigate its workings through observable behavior.

The social learning paradigm basically views learning as a continuous process rather than a series of stages. The concept is a type of behaviorism, but differs in several key respects. Whereas strict behaviorism assumes that a response must be performed and reinforced before it can be considered to have been learned, social learning theory states that learning can also occur as a result of observation. Observational learning is said to occur in a four-step sequence: *Attention* is given, by watching or listening, to a "model" performing the behavior to be learned. *Retention* of the behavior occurs in memory. *Motor reproduction* of the behavior converts the symbols stored in memory into the act itself. And, *motivation* persuades the subject not just that he or she can perform the act, but to get on with actually doing it (Bandura, 1976). This theory accepts that conditioning, reward, and punishment all contribute to social development, but asserts that children learn by observation as well and that this type of learning can take place without any direct reward or punishment at all.

An acceptable way of investigating consciousness from the social learning paradigmatic viewpoint could be based on the "standard" method—developing hypotheses, empirically testing the hypotheses, and then revising and refining the hypotheses. But cognitive social learning also lends itself to observational research techniques, in which the subjects are observed during their everyday lives in their natural environment. The observers (researchers) remain unobtrusive so as not to interfere with the natural behavior of the subjects being observed, simultaneously sampling several behaviors in a single-subject, baseline design to provide multiple baselines of behavior (those that are natural). Consequently, a tentative explanation for any phenomenon observed will be based on objective observation and logic, and subject to empirical tests (Bordens and Abbott, 1991).

Experimental and Observational Methodologies

Let us now look more closely at these two alternative methods for studying consciousness. This should help to give an even clearer understanding of the reasons for choosing hermeneutics as the tool of scrutiny for the study of such an elusive topic. Although researchers in human behavior hold differing views of the exact meaning of "experimental," most would agree that an experiment is a recording of observations of specified operations under defined conditions. Even this minimal requirement would be a little difficult to accomplish when relating to consciousness. For example, under this method, one generally needs to select variables to compare which lend themselves to observation and measurement. There is also the requirement to limit experimental events to those which can be controlled, manipulated, or held constant (Borg and Gall, 1989). Then there is the necessity for control groups, random assignment of participants to conditions, and the use of statistical analyses which organize observations in a form permitting meaningful inference and interpretation.

The main purpose of experimental method is to establish a cause-and-effect relationship between two variables, thereby explaining the effect. How would one do this when studying consciousness? The experimental method is best chosen when the question posed for investigation can be addressed through the manipulation and control of events. When only the magnitude and cause of the effect are at issue, the experimental method is usually the preferred means of investigation.

One also has to consider such things as design, procedures, and analyses. There are five general characteristics of research designs classified as experimental. These are "specificity of variables," that is, being quite clear on all the experimental variables; the use of control groups; random assignment of participants; control of conditions; and the interpretation of cause and effect (Dallmayr and McCarthy, 1977).

Basically, experimental research designs are intended to bring forth observations which represent the groups and treatment conditions used in a particular study. The researcher must be able to select appropriate means of analyzing the data received. It is obvious that it would be hard to determine what tangible data could be received from the entity we refer to as consciousness. There could possibly be ways to extract useful information pertaining to human general awareness from the standard scientific method, but it is easy to see that it would not be the first choice in many cases. The observational method of human inquiry may turn out to be a little more useful. It is perhaps the oldest type of research in human history. As the name implies, this method simply involves continual observation of people going about their everyday activities, over a prolonged period of time, in what would be considered their natural habitat. This can include special events like celebrations and festivals as well as unexpected events and crises. The investigator attempts to objectively record the course of happenings and relations among events and people. This method would seem to be more useful in the study of human thought, mind, awareness, and consciousness.

The main purpose of this method is to allow the investigator to put together information which points to a description of people in general and any patterns and relationships among these people and the events that surround their lives (Borg and Gall, 1989). This research path could possibly give up some interesting information about the correlation between certain aspects of perceptions of reality and the interpretations of those perceptions in consciousness. One of the main reasons for this is that the method is chiefly descriptive; descriptions are always intertwined with meaning and, as we have noted before, *meaning* is a major ingredient in the understanding of anything done by humans.

It is logical that the emphasis in the observational approach to research is on the natural setting and on studying that setting as it naturally occurs. Standard research designs that fit into the natural setting would be hard to conceive in the majority of cases. In fact, such a design can often be counterproductive to the main purpose for the research. However, the observational method retains the option of using some empirical elements, and leaves room for introducing questions and hypotheses, which can be formulated and put forth just as with any method of data collection.

Our investigation of the behavioral and cognitive theoretical paradigms and the experimental and observational research methodologies leads us to the following questions: How much actual control do we really have over our own personal lives and actions? How much of what we do in our day-to-day living is controlled by behavior? How much introspection, insight, and free choice is really involved? What is the result of independent, conscious thought and what is externally manipulated? An important adjunct to these issues of control is a major question about consciousness itself: is consciousness (feelings, emotions, memory, insight, etc.) uniquely human? Or is consciousness a matter of degree? If a dog has one half our brain mass, does it have one half our consciousness? If a frog has a thousandth of our brain mass, does it have a thousandth of our consciousness? One could probably arrive at interesting answers to these questions using either the behaviorist or the social learning theory paradigm, the experimental or the observational method. But whether they would be the "correct" answers is another question altogether.

When doing research it is always helpful to remember that the truth is what *is* so about something—the reality of the matter—as opposed to what people wish were so, believe to be so, or assert to be so. No matter how long and loud we may shout, "This is the truth," and no matter how deeply we may believe what we say, the truth of the matter is not changed one bit (Ruggiero, 1984). What we perceive to be true may change. What we perceive to be reality may be altered. However, the truth is, was, and shall always be the truth. Now, having said that, we should also acknowledge the fact that, in anything and everything, there is probably more than one truth.

To reiterate, the main reason for the current questioning of the "standard view" of research is concern over its methodological bias against adequate human studies, especially pertaining to such areas as consciousness. The growing weight of information strengthens the belief that the human dimension adds new ingredients which now call for new methods of investigation. In this endeavor, hermeneutics shows itself as the discipline of choice.

CHAPTER 2

The Brain

Beginnings

The majority of scientists who study the origins of the universe would most likely pick the "Big Bang" theory as offering the best available explanation of what actually happened. This theory of cosmogony posits that the universe began at a single, tiny point of immense heat and density, experienced an incomparable explosion, and has been expanding ever since. According to the theory, right after the explosion the universe was only about a centimeter across. No one knows exactly how large it is now, but its hugeness is difficult for the human mind to fully understand. For example, it is believed that traveling at the speed of light (186,000 miles per second), it would take about ten years just to get to the nearest star in our own galaxy! There are millions of stars farther away in our galaxy, and there are millions of other galaxies in the universe (Snow, 1985).

To even begin to investigate the current universe, it is necessary to make certain assumptions. These assumptions, in principle at least, should be testable. However, it is certainly not clear at this time how one could practically go about doing such testing. (Here, of course, there is a correlation with the study of consciousness.) An astronomer often has to act as philosopher, and make a priori assumptions. One fairly traditional assumption is that the universe must be "homogeneous," that is to say, that the density and general structure of galaxies must be constant. This is not known for certain, but many indications are that the universe does seem to be formulated in this manner.

The most basic questions pertaining to the universe remain unanswered, and the complexities involved in answering them are enormous. Even if one accepts the Big Bang theory, the initial question of how the universe began is not really answered. Let us say there actually was a tiny speck with all that mass and energy packed into it, which then exploded and expanded into what we have before us now. That still leaves a very important question: where did the speck come from?

Our solar system is believed to have been formed about five billion years ago, about ten billion years after the Big Bang, from the collapse of rotating interstellar clouds. The space debris first condensed around an infant sun and then coalesced into the nine planets within our system. Geological evidence indicates that the earth is a little more than four billion years old (Sagan, 1980). During the first billion years of its existence, the earth was mostly a molten mass. Then the elements began to separate and the densest materials, such as iron, sank to the core. At the same time, volatile gases formed the earliest atmosphere, primarily composed of hydrogen, ammonia, methane, and water vapor.

The first forms of life on earth probably evolved about one billion years ago (Shapiro, 1987). According to archaeological data, the first pre-humans, or hominids, seem to have appeared between two and three million years ago. A somewhat higher form of hominid, *Homo erectus*, came onto the scene about one and a half million years ago, followed by *Homo habilis* and others, until *Homo sapiens neanderthalensis*, better known as Neanderthal man, arose between one and two hundred thousand years ago—the first hominid considered to belong to the same species as you and I. However, what we refer to as "modern man," no different from human beings of today, is believed to have come into existence only about 50 to 75 thousand years ago (Asimov, 1987).

How and when something as ethereal and abstract as consciousness "began" is a question of astounding reach. Beginnings of anything are hard to pinpoint, especially in relation to the complex questions we are considering here. It is a good idea to keep in mind at all times that the "answers" offered by the most esteemed scientists are still opinions—educated ones, to be sure, but opinions nevertheless. This lack of absolute certainty applies as much to the "beginnings" of the human species as it does to any other inquiry. The search for answers about the "beginnings" of the universe, the galaxies, the solar system, the earth, life, and human life is as closely correlated to the investigation of consciousness as starting is connected to finishing. Where does the human species go from here? This is the point where specific consciousness studies come into play. It is essential to know where one has been in order to determine where one might be going. Knowledge of the evolutionary beginnings of everything, including the universe itself, is helpful in formulating ideas about the potential for the future of the human animal — both as a species and as individuals.

An integral part of this investigation relates to the mind-body problem discussed in the last chapter. That is, what is the specific correlation between brain and mind, and is it possible for mind to have any autonomy from brain? Where is the "mind"? What does it "look" like? Does it have mass? Is it measurable? Is it separate from the brain at all? It could be stated that the spatial proximity of brain to mind has direct correlation to the responsibility of neuron transmissions. The more basic the endeavor by the nervous system, the less connected to the mind that endeavor would be; the farther away from foundational biological functions — those that simply sustain life — the more the mind would come into play. According to this view, neuron responsibility for regulating the heartbeat would be in extremely close proximity to tangible brain matter. Voluntary motor activity would involve a lesser, but still quite close, proximity to the biological brain mass. Intelligence and nearly all decision making processes would be partly the result of brain mechanisms and partly the result of autonomous manifestations of mind. The most extreme separation would have to do with self-awareness, which contains all of the most creative departments within what we call consciousness. It is in this last area where the mind reaches its highest potential for full independence from the brain.

The Biological Brain

Philosophers and scientists have been theorizing about the functions and nature of the brain since Hippocrates located the center of thought within the head. The scope of the chemical and electrical activity within the brain that controls memory, creative potential, and automatic processes is as extensive and mysterious as any galaxy in the known universe. The brain, as well as the mind, as we have seen, can be viewed from so many standpoints that generalizations are virtually impossible. The maze of the brain is too complex for even the most brilliant scientists to comprehend to any great degree.

The human brain can be represented by making two fists. It is a two-sided, walnut-shaped compendium of nearly 12 billion cells. Weighing slightly over three pounds, it is an undefined series of lumps and lines of pinkish gray matter with the texture of soft, unprocessed cheese. Millions of pieces of information are mysteriously stored in this comparatively small area. Here our autonomic, or involuntary, bodily functions are unconsciously organized and regulated (Lilly, 1982). Thousands of chemical and electrical actions take place within the smallest measurable fraction of a second. The brain's multi-dimensional functions also encompass the somewhat separate entity known as "mind." The information within the mind engages in endless interplay, projecting dreams onto a nocturnal video screen, composing unique aspects of behavior and personality, and manufacturing the endless variety of learning, responding, and feeling which constitute our unique human nature—defining, in other words, what it is to be human.

In the adult brain, there are more than ten trillion nerve cells, comprising what could be called a small computer, programmed by a combination of chemicals and electricity. Most of these cells, called neurons, are formed by the end of the first year of life. Since they do not divide like other cells, they cannot replace themselves (Farthing, 1992). It is a curious fact that nearly 10,000 of these neurons die each day after the age of 21, so that the weight of the brain actually decreases with age. That, however, does not seem to be an important factor in the loss of overall mental abilities.

Most neurons can link up with an average of about 60,000 other neurons, resulting in approximately one quadrillion possible connections. Each neuron has three parts: the cell body, the axon, and the dendrites. These are roughly comparable to the trunk, roots, and branches of a tree. Through chemical and electrical charges, caused by a combination of sodium and potassium, the neurons send signals to one another. Each neuron seems to send exactly the same type of electrical signal, varying its frequency depending on the intensity of the experience. When an electrical signal leaves a neuron, it passes through the axon. It fires a chemical called a neurotransmitter across a gap, called a synapse, to the receptive dendrite of another neuron. This triggers another electrical signal in the neighboring neuron, which in turn produces another neurotransmitter.

Electrical activity in the brain occurs in four wave forms, each of which operates at certain speeds, or frequencies. Beta waves are the most common type found in our normal, conscious states. These waves vibrate at between 18 and 40 cycles per second. This type of activity is mostly recorded in the frontal and parietal regions of the cerebral cortex. Alpha waves are most commonly found when one is quiet and resting. Usually the eyes are closed and there is no problem solving taking place. The alpha waves occupy the frequency range of 8 to 12 cycles per second. Third are theta waves, which are observed mainly in the temporal and parietal regions of children's brains and occasionally in adults experiencing great stress from disappointment or frustration. They can also be observed in states of high creativity. These waves undulate at four to seven cycles per second. Finally there are delta waves, found in very deep states of sleep, with frequencies of one to three cycles per second. Breathing is deep and the blood pressure decreases, as well as the heartbeat and body temperature. This state is unconscious and thus is the least understood (Rosenthal, 1991).

The brain cells are kept alive and functioning by oxygen, which is brought to the brain by blood. While the brain makes up approximately 2 percent of the body's weight, it consumes from 19 to 25 percent of the body's oxygen. In all other parts of the body, the amount of blood oxygen is directly proportional to the amount of physical work done. The brain receives 20 percent of all the blood that is pumped from the heart and regulates its own flow. The more blood and oxygen there is in the brain, the more intellectual activity seems to increase. The brain is both a sending and a receiving agent for the nervous system. The conversion of thought to physical action passes through hundreds of networks, jumping the spaces between the neurons and relaying messages simultaneously from the senses at varying speeds. Depending on the familiarity of the action, the sending of these messages and the responses to them can travel from 300 to 400 miles an hour (Tarcher, 1983).

The Mechanics of the Brain

Different portions of the brain, of course, process different experiences simultaneously. The lowest portions of the brain take care of the physical systems of the body. The largest part of this lower brain is the cerebellum, which is the coordinating area for muscle movement. It works on an autonomic, subconscious level to keep the higher portions of the brain informed of the motions of the fingers, feet, arms, and legs, and all other voluntary motor movements. The brain stem serves as the cable which carries information to and from the rest of the body via the spinal cord.

In other specific areas of brain function, the hypothalamus regulates the temperature of the body and the desire for food and governs pain, depression, and pleasure responses. The hippocampus develops short-term memory and prepares messages for other parts of the brain to store information permanently. The basal ganglia regulate balance and bodily movement. The amygdala is a processing place for old memories and habits as they travel to the cerebral cortex. The thalamus receives information from the senses and relays the information to different areas of the cortex (Springer and Deutsch, 1989).

The cortex is the covering of the brain and is the large area that controls our intelligence and higher mental activities. This area is most developed in dolphins and humans. Here sensations, experienced and registered as voluntary actions, are initiated. It has been called the seat of our humanity because of its ability to store facts as memory. Here we make decisions and formulate logic. And it is here that we firmly center the arena of our awareness, or consciousness.

The cortex is divided into two lobes or hemispheres, each processing a different kind of information. These two lobes are connected by a network of hundreds of thousands of small fibers called the corpus callosum. Much of the popular attention given to the brain in recent years has emphasized these two lobes, calling them the "left" and "right" brain. This classification makes it easier for the learner to understand a variety of mental processes. However, there are more portions of the cerebral cortex than just the generalized right and left lobes.

Three more specific lobes are found within the cortex. The parietal lobe receives information which can interpret special details and sensory stimuli; it selects which information coming into the brain will be attended to and processed. The temporal lobe is the center of hearing and of the memory of information communicated through sound. The frontal lobe, or neo-cortex, is evolutionarily the newest part of the brain and the most highly developed. It can conceive of the future, plan in advance, and set overall goals; it can also relate to such concepts as altruism (Ackerman, 1992).

Another area of the cortex, which extends around the top of the head and toward the top of the ears, responds to the sensory functions of the body. This area is called the sensory homunculus (the word means "little man"). It receives the impressions of touch and physical motion. The sensory area on the right side receives information from the left side of the body and the area on the left receives information from the right side of the body. Large areas in this section of the brain are activated by the mouth, lips, and fingers. The amount of cortex area devoted to each of the various sensory detectors is determined by their use.

The motor homunculus runs parallel to the sensory homunculus. It is the sending station, controlling the physical activities of the body. Large areas are given to the thumbs, fingers, hands, and head. These areas are important in the learning process. When they are stimulated, the brain is awakened to more potential. Multisensory integration can take place in these areas (Adelman, 1987). That said, it must of course be added that the brain is so complex and interconnected that it is difficult to separate its functions and areas into these simple generalizations.

In most animals the structure of the nervous system is essentially symmetrical. In mammals this symmetry is made more striking by the prominence of the top portion of the brain, the cerebral hemispheres. In humans, however, the two cerebral hemispheres differ greatly in their functions. The left hemisphere plays a dominant role in speech and verbal skills and the right hemisphere plays a dominant role in emotion and perceptions of our environment (Springer and Deutsch, 1989). For more than a century the principal source of knowledge about the division of labor between the two cerebral hemispheres of the human brain has been malfunctions of the brain caused by accident, surgery, or disease. Although research on intellectual impairments in patients with various kinds of brain lesions have provided much useful information, such studies are disadvantaged by the fact that the damage may have affected not only the specific functional systems but also their interactions.

A peculiarity of the human nervous system is that each cerebral hemisphere receives data primarily from the opposite half of the body. The visual, tactile, and motor systems of the brain are almost completely crossed. This is quite interesting in a number of different ways, but whether it has an impact on consciousness and its particular workings is not known at this time.

There is evidence indicating that the separation of the hemispheres creates two independent spheres of consciousness within a single cranium, that is to say, within a single organism. This conclusion is still controversial. It is disturbing to some people who view consciousness as an indivisible property of the human brain. It seems premature to others, who insist that present knowledge reveals that the capacities of the right hemisphere are those of an automaton. But according to this new evidence, it is entirely possible that if the brain of a very young person were divided, both hemispheres could separately and independently develop mental functions of a high order, at a level attained only in the left hemisphere of normal individuals.

As we have seen, the sensory and motor functions of the brain are fairly well known. Studies by neurologists and psychologists over the past century have located the centers responsible for some elementary functions such as seeing, hearing, and the control of the body's muscular systems. In order to proceed further with the mapping of the brain's functions we must continue to look into the systems responsible for the higher, more complex behavioral processes. However, when we consider many of the highest processes and even potential processes of the mind and of consciousness, it seems that the rapid evolution of modern society is outpacing the mind's capacity to keep up with the blazing speed of environmental changes. We have reached consciousness overload and the lines separating what is logical and what is illogical, what is reality and what is not reality have become quite undefined.

How connected with body is mind? To go further, how connected with mind is consciousness? We know that, to a large extent, mind is created biologically, that its manifestation is powered by the electrical and chemical "fuel" available in the brains of all higher animals. Further up the evolutionary ladder, so to speak, a "higher" mind, or consciousness, comes into being. However, are these "inter" workings totally necessary throughout the entire existence of individual consciousness, or is the need only of a contemporary nature? That is to say, can consciousness be formulated and fueled, wholly or in part, by other means as well? If so, what are these other means? Philosophers and scientists alike have been struggling to resolve this split between substance and psyche since they first became conscious of the problematic question in the first place.

CHAPTER 3

Multiple Consciousness

A thorough investigation of the literature can give us a solid understanding of previous contributions to the study of consciousness. This, in turn, leads us to a better understanding of how to study consciousness, through a consideration of past methods of inquiry and newer, perhaps more workable, methods of inquiry. That was the task of Chapter 1. The process also, of course, should lead to the development of new, more useful ideas about what the definition(s) of consciousness might be. This allows for a more pragmatic investigation and the possibility of more useful outcomes.

The most cursory inspection of any number of books and articles written on the subject of consciousness reveals the ambiguous and somewhat controversial nature of its multiplicity of potential meanings. In-depth inquiry exposes the ongoing contention quite blatantly.

Normal States of Consciousness

In an attempt to order and clarify the subject, Thomas Natsoulas (1978) places the differing states of consciousness under seven basic headings: joint or mutual knowledge, internal knowledge or conviction, awareness, direct awareness, personal unity, the normal waking state, and double consciousness.

Joint or mutual knowledge is described by Natsoulas as a sharing of information with one or more other persons. Something that two or more people are aware of could be described as joint consciousness. In an addendum to his original study (1983), Natsoulas clarifies this state as a "kind of cognitive relation between people" (p. 121). He gives as an example "an exchange of knowing glances." For instance, when two female companions notice an attractive man walk into a room, they might simultaneously turn and look into each other's eyes, each "knowing" what the other is thinking.

Internal knowledge or conviction is defined by Natsoulas as knowledge that is first-hand, that is, information known in the most personal way. It is not necessary that anyone else share this knowledge, and if they did their awareness would be second-hand. Only the initial "knower" is intimately aware of it, because he or she was the initiator and developer of this knowledge in the first place. Natsoulas (1978) further clarifies his point by stating this second concept as "sharing knowledge with myself about myself" (p. 910). To give an example: I am in a courtroom testifying under oath. I know that I am telling the truth. Others may believe I am being truthful, but I know myself within myself, and only I am capable of that knowledge.

Awareness, as defined by Natsoulas, simply means being aware of something, anything—awareness in the present tense. One can be aware that one is thinking, walking, talking, going to the movies, about to be killed, and so on. It doesn't matter how the awareness is being produced or what the basic foundation of the awareness is, only that it is. For example, I am typing at this moment. I am aware of that action. That is an example of general awareness.

Direct awareness can be said to be "perception of an inward psychological fact" (Natsoulas, 1978, p. 911). This would be a knowledge that is intrinsic, endemic, or intuitive. To experience direct awareness is to have a thought that is automatically understood as fact—it is "the truth." I am watching a bird drink water from a pond in my back yard at this very moment. It is a personally known truth. I am directly aware that it is happening now.

Personal unity seems to be one of the more difficult spheres of consciousness. It is said to be the sum total of one's thoughts, feelings, and impressions. This would also include past experiences and events that may be intertwined with others' consciousness. But Natsoulas (1978) goes on to say that the most potentially correct understanding of the process may pertain to viewing unity consciousness as something that is achieved. It may not be entirely relevant that some events come from outside and some from within. "All one's mental episodes are one's own because they occur in the same organism" (Natsoulas, 1983, p. 121). Unity is achieved through the individual's personal point of view. The totality is more than just the sum of the stream of mental episodes; one must make them one's own. This concept could, in fact, relate to a kind of constructivism.

That is, from my viewpoint, your behavior is my perception. It may not be at all what you intended, but it is what I perceive that you intended (Hoffman, 1988). What I perceive to be is my reality; my reality is the only thing that matters to me. An example might be three different people watching a political debate among three candidates. They all watch the same thing, but at the end one says X won, one says Y won, and one says Z won. In part, at least, these viewpoints are the result of both contemporary data and mental impressions from past experience.

The normal waking state should not be confused with a general state of consciousness (Natsoulas, 1978). A number of possible altered states of consciousness can occur within the general state, e.g., a thought process that could take place while awake or while dreaming. The normal waking state corresponds to being absolutely wide awake and attentive to the task at hand. In order to disarm a live bomb, one would need to be in the waking state of consciousness.

Double consciousness refers to the possibility of more than a single consciousness—that is, more than one train of thought or mental capability—within a single person. This could also be described as more than one personality. Self-deception has been put forward as a possible example of this double consciousness (Natsoulas, 1978). A more specific example is a person perceiving that the same thing is and is not true, that something happened and did not happen. Further, Natsoulas (1983) refers to double consciousness as "two coexisting consciousnesses, in the same person" (p. 122). A more concrete possibility relating to this concept could pertain to one of the well-known partitions of schizophrenia. The essential features of this disorder are the presence of certain psychotic symptoms during the active phase of the illness. Some of the symptoms are delusions, hallucinations, and peculiar behavior such as hoarding food or talking to inanimate objects. It is possible that these could be tangible examples of double consciousness in disarray.

As we attempt further investigation into consciousness in the future, one of the main stumbling blocks to avoid will be peripheral inquiry on multitudes of sub-levels. Answers about the what, why, and how of consciousness need to be based on some kind of general consensus as to its basic, foundational definition. This definition has to encompass the points of view of both the natural sciences and the human sciences. However, at present the disparity between different concepts of consciousness appears to be quite broad even within disciplines, although consensus does seem more elusive among those on the psychological side than among those who espouse the neurological approach. Nevertheless, it is better to be vaguely correct than clearly incorrect.

An approach to explaining consciousness that is similar, but not identical, to Natsoulas's is that of G. William Farthing (1992), who simply states that it is "the fundamental fact of human existence" (p. 1). This relates to persons' direct awareness of their own experiences. We can, in fact, only be aware of our own consciousness. It would be impossible to be aware, first-hand, of someone else's consciousness. This particular line of thought is very similar to the philosophic constructivist point of view, that other people's behavior is our experience and can never be otherwise (Hoffman, 1988). This viewpoint asserts the need to change from an *observed* system (about others) to an *observing* system (about ourselves). We can never really know what is "out there." The only thing we have even a small chance of knowing is what is "inside."

Consciousness is a part of mind, but is not mind (Farthing, 1992). Farthing goes on to state that mind is "the functioning of the brain to process information and control action in a flexible and adaptive manner" (p. 5). But consciousness is much more difficult to pin down in words. The concept is something we must understand intuitively. Let us add a few more layers of difficulty. Natsoulas (1978, 1983) lists seven separate types of consciousness. Farthing (1992) puts consciousness under four separate headings, and adds sub-levels under those headings. Some of the headings are similar to Natsoulas's, for example, awareness and wakefulness. Others are somewhat different, such as executive control systems and reflective consciousness. The "executive control system" of consciousness is responsible for the direct and overall control of the complete brain/mind system. Reflective consciousness is the exercise of thinking about one's personal experiences.

Another similar but still slightly different explanation calls consciousness "a domain of internalized motion, an insight into oneself as a moving experience" (Fischer, 1986, p. 3). Fischer goes on to relate mental activities in a more natural science vein, as tangible muscular acts that can be detected with electromyographic recordings, and introduces such related topics as "sensory-motor closure," "synapse circuits," and the cartography of non-ordinary states of consciousness.

Altered States of Consciousness

Beyond the major challenges of attempting to understand and more specifically define the areas of normal consciousness, we must also consider the goodly number of altered states of consciousness (ASCs), sub-areas that fall under the general umbrella of consciousness. Popular interest in ASCs has increased more rapidly than scholarly understanding of this topic. Nevertheless, a considerable variety of material has emerged, primarily concerning such areas as sleep and dream states, psychedelic drug experience, meditation, biofeedback, hypnosis, suggestion, fantasy, and pseudomemory. Let us now look at the first four of these in detail; the others will be discussed in the next chapter.

The nocturnal *dream* can be considered an ASC of universal occurrence among humans and other primates (Krippner, 1990). Despite an ancient psychosocial and psychological preoccupation with the symbolic content of dreams, research in the field has only in the past few decades acquired respectable scientific status (Krippner and Dillard, 1988). There is the notorious problem of the "bad witness factor" in verbal reports of dreaming, as the investigator is not sure how accurately the dream has been reported or, indeed, if the subject dreamed at all. Further, psychoanalytic interpretations of symbolic dream content often appear to be arbitrary and do not meet the falsifiability criterion of scientific work. Nevertheless, there has been much argument for the importance of first-person viewpoints.

For thousands of years, probably since well before recorded history, people have been fascinated by dreams. The emotional impact of dreams can be so powerful that it seems unlikely that they are a completely accidental or trivial phenomenon. The attribution of meaning to dreams has taken different forms in different times and different cultures. People in some cultures have believed dreams are messages from the gods, or that they predict the future. In the modern Western world, people who study the field believe that dreams reveal profoundly important aspects of the dreamer's personality. This point of view is most strong in psychoanalysis.

The discovery by Aserinsky and Kleitman (1953) that dream reports could be elicited by waking a sleeping subject immediately following the observation of rapid eye movements (REMs) permitted investigators to study important but previously neglected phenomena. Unless one is drunk, drugged, or brain-damaged, one will have about four or five REM periods each night, interspersed with periods of three other sleep stages, each with a physiologically distinct signature on an electroencephalogram (EEG). Although modern instrumentation can record the "mechanics" of a dream in progress, the only way researchers can know about people's actual dreams is through their verbal introspective reports. The drawback is that dream reports are, of course, subject to all of the limitations of introspective reporting described earlier in reference to consciousness itself. Dreaming is a subjective experience; the dreamer is the only person who can "know" the dream. Even if we try to explain our dreams we are subject to such things as forgetting, construction errors, and verbal description difficulties.

Among the most dramatic altered states of consciousness are those produced by *psychoactive drugs*. Psychedelic drugs, in particular, have been used to produce altered states that will, the user hopes, enhance self-understanding, creativity, or mystical experience, or, failing that, provide entertainment, albeit with certain risks attached. (A psychoactive drug is one which alters brain function in *any* way. A psychedelic drug is just one of that category.)

The alterations in consciousness associated with psychosis (e.g., manic-depressive disorder, the schizophrenias) and the use of psychedelic drugs (e.g., LSD, psilocybin, mescaline, hashish) have provided masses of phenomenological experience which has been extensively described but poorly accounted for by theory. Although progress has been made in describing the specific neuropharmacology of both psychoses and psychedelics, no behavioral, physiological, or linguistic account has provided a unified explanation of the specific contents of these altered states (Dobkin de Rios, 1984).

Basically, psychoactive drugs affect consciousness and behavior by modifying the process of "synaptic transmission" in the brain. Excitatory and inhibitory connections between neurons are carried out through the transfer of special biochemicals, called neurotransmitters, across the tiny synaptic gap between neurons. Different kinds of neurotransmitters are present in different parts or circuits of the brain, and the psychological effects of a given drug will depend upon which particular neurotransmitter it affects and how it affects it (McKim, 1986).

It may be well to note that any feeling possible to our human nervous system may be aroused in the psychedelic state. This applies not only to familiar feelings but also to very early preverbal feeling states. Also characteristic of the influence of hallucinogens are, of course, the well-known ecstatic states, as well as counter-ecstatic states, which are to grief what ecstasy is to ordinary happiness and pleasure.

A third area generally considered to be an altered state of consciousness is *meditation*. The forms of meditation are many and varied, but all involve a training and self-regulation of attention. Goleman (1977) has broadly classified these forms as "concentration," "insight," and "interactive." Some meditation practices associated with Eastern spiritual traditions include bhakti, the ecstatic union with the divine (concentration); jhana, which emphasizes discrimination through wisdom (interactive); tantra, involving repetitions of mantras and contemplation of mandalas (concentration); the mindfulness or attentiveness of the Buddhist traditions (interactive); the Gurdjieff method of self-remembrance (insight); and Krishnamurti's philosophy of self-knowledge (insight) (Krippner and Malisewski, 1978).

Why do people meditate? The goals of meditation mostly fall into two categories: religious and secular. The religious meditation tradition is at least 2,500 years old, and it includes most religions. The secular meditation tradition, which is relatively new, includes the use of meditation to improve one's sense of well-being, for example, by gaining personal insight, increasing creativity, or coping with the stress of life's daily hassles and major transitions. Secular meditation may be a form of self-therapy or part of a directed psychotherapy program (Carrington, 1977).

Formal meditation usually occurs only when certain minimal conditions have been met, but the mood or emotional tone that underlies the meditative state is familiar to everyone and constitutes one of the most appreciated of human experiences. This meditative mood usually occurs quite spontaneously and is marked by its ephemeral nature (Carrington, 1977). Recognized at once as a moment of unusual aliveness, or perhaps of inner illumination, it can include some of the profoundly positive ASCs that Maslow (1962) referred to as "peak experiences" and is often indistinguishable from the moments of inner stillness intentionally evoked by the ritual of meditation.

Some aspects of the physiology of meditation have been relatively well studied (Shapiro, 1987). Yogis and Zen monks have been shown to be able to decrease their oxygen consumption voluntarily.

Fakirs can adopt tortuous postures with their bodies and can demonstrate remarkable control of their autonomic organs. Control of breath (prana) is known to be a fundamental aspect of successful meditation. Yogis practicing concentration show EEG synchronization of predominantly high-frequency beta waves between the cerebral hemispheres, as well as an increase in alpha waves. Zen monks, who practice an open-eyed form of meditation know as za-zen, show a predominance of alpha waves, although alpha ordinarily tends to increase with the eyes closed (Dillbeck, Banus, Polanzi, and Landrith, 1988).

The field of *biofeedback* has grown rapidly since its initial popularization in the late 1960s. It has been extravagantly hailed as a major breakthrough in the health sciences and criticized as an overpackaged, oversold placebo with little scientific validity. Both viewpoints have diminished, and now a more realistic assessment of biofeedback is emerging. As a research tool, biofeedback promises to answer difficult questions about the relationship between mental and physiological variables because it affords the possibility of voluntary control of the involuntary, or autonomic, nervous system. Further, it offers the possibility of defining and exploring states of consciousness with a rigorous methodology (Kamiya, 1971).

Biofeedback is simply the feedback to a person of biological information about his or her bodily workings. It is the continuous monitoring, amplifying, and displaying to a person (usually by a needle on a meter, or by a light or a tone) of the ongoing internal physiological processes, such as muscle tension, temperature, heart behavior, or brain rhythm. Biofeedback is not conditioning, and it is not therapy, any more than the act of looking at one's weight on a bathroom scale is conditioning or therapy.

The clinical application of biofeedback has met with varied but significant success in a large number of psychosomatic disorders. The management of stress and hypertension is perhaps the most common application of electromyograph (EMG) and alpha biofeedback. These techniques, as well as others dealing with pain management, alcoholism treatment, sex therapy, athletic training, and pediatric and geriatric applications, are most effectively used with a general therapeutic paradigm called self-regulation. Self-regulatory procedures are being increasingly applied in counseling and psychotherapy, where the sense of self plays an important therapeutic role (Sarnoff, 1982).

It is now clear to most therapists that clinical biofeedback training, if it is to be effective, involves first and foremost the conscious volition of the client, and secondarily the conscious volition of the trainer. This discredits the belief of many early researchers that the left cortex of the trainer's brain was essential to success in training clients, but that neither the left nor the right cerebral cortex of the patient needed to be consciously involved, any more than in a deep trance state.

Psychic Phenomena

Anomalous psychological experiences which seem to contradict orthodox scientific concepts of space, time, and energy are among the most interesting phenomena reported by those experiencing ASCs (Wolman and Ullman, 1986). Such phenomena are generically known as "psi." However, because the prevailing world view of Western science rejects the possible reality of such phenomena a priori, psi research has remained on the front lines of a "paradigm clash" since its inception. While its advocates take the view that the range of psi phenomena may be vastly important for the scientific understanding of human nature, mainstream science dismisses psi as non-repeatable and inexplicable (e.g., Druckman and Swet, 1988). In the face of these negative attitudes, researchers in parapsychology have attempted to be extremely careful, thorough, and scrupulous in their methods. As a result, they have established a body of evidence which they claim supports the existence of several varieties of psi effects (Krippner, 1990). Nonetheless, critics of psi point out that after 100 years of research, not a single individual has been found who can demonstrate psi on demand to the satisfaction of independent investigators.

Parapsychology is the scientific study of psi phenomena, defined as interactions between organisms and their environment which defy explanation in terms of current scientific paradigms. Some of the major categories of psi are clairvoyance, precognition, telepathy, psychokinesis, and mysticism. Parapsychologists also study paranormal healing and reports of survival of the human personality following bodily death (Irwin, 1989).

The first group to devote itself to the scientific study of psi was the Society for Psychical Research, organized in London in 1882.

Its members were especially interested in studying life after death, ghosts, and mediums (Kelly and Locke, 1981). Hypnosis was a frequent topic of investigation and discussion. In 1885, the American Society for Psychical Research was founded; here, too, an active interest was taken in mediums and in the information they produced through their "spirit controls" while in altered conscious states.

It is important to separate the question of the causes of mystical states of consciousness from the question of the truth or validity of the insights that occur to people in such states. Science can judge the truth of mystical insights only insofar as they make claims that can be studied by scientific methods, which is rarely the case. Mystical insights are more likely to be in the realm of faith than in the realm of science. Whether someone's mystical insights are valued by others or interpreted as signs of insanity, delusion, or fraud often depends upon the particular culture in which they occur.

CHAPTER 4

"Recovered Memory"

Four related altered states of consciousness are hypnosis, suggestion, fantasy, and pseudomemory. These phenomena act and interact together, and thus are discussed collectively in this chapter, particularly as regards their relationship to the controversial phenomenon of "recovered memory." This is an area where very real negative elements frequently come into play.

The immediate present, or "now," is already past at the very moment we are aware of it. This is so because of the approximately 60 to 70 milliseconds of processing by the nervous system that has to precede our awareness of "now" (Efron, 1967). Moreover, "being" at each moment is structured through memory, and what we perceive as the present is a vivid fringe of memory tinged with anticipation. Accordingly, the "being" of present always resides in a past. The intense condensation of this past and its representation is the flashback: "In a second, the faintest perfume may send us plummeting to the roots of our being; by a mere smell we are connected to another place and another time" (Purce, 1974, p. 3).

Remembering is a conscious experience. We can distinguish between memory, as a flexible system in which information is stored, and remembering, or recollection, as the conscious experience that accompanies retrieval of information from the memory system. Memory is one of the two sources of information input to consciousness, the other source being the sensory systems. Remembering involves conscious mental images, often accompanied by inner speech, which represent the knowledge of past personal events.

In separate experiments conducted on rats and humans, researchers have found the first direct evidence that memories are consolidated during sleep. Parts of these studies noted that when an animal moved through a somewhat familiar environment, a particular pattern of cells was activated in a part of the brain called the hippocampus. Soon afterward, when the animals were allowed to sleep, the same cells showed an increased tendency to fire at the same time. It was hypothesized that this occurs as the memories are being consolidated in the brain. There is additional evidence that those persons who have a positive attitude toward dreaming tend to report better recall of their dreams than less fantasy-prone people (Tonay, 1993).

In considering the various forms of mental images, Sheikh and Shaffer (1979) distinguish the following: visual afterimages, which move or disappear with saccadic eye movement; memory images, which a subject typically describes in the past tense; imagination images, including hypnagogic, or daydream images; and eidetic images, which are characterized by clarity and detail, are reported in the present tense, and superimposed to produce composite images. Several researchers have taken an interest in hypnagogic fantasy as a technique to gain access to the unconscious. Shepard and Cooper (1982), and later Bornstein (1978), confirmed that before carrying out a physical operation or task, people often first imagine how they would perform it.

It is when hypnosis, suggestion, fantasy, and pseudomemory come into play simultaneously that a negative with potentially severe consequences begins to expose itself. Even under therapeutic auspices, the power of suggestion on perception, thinking, and memory can be strong. Subjectively, these can be the most dramatically "influenced" experiences. This is of particular concern because the most important practical applications of strong suggestion or hypnosis involve the patient's responses to posthypnotic suggestions to achieve cognitive changes during and after therapy.

Hypnosis

The promise of hypnosis as a means of studying the psychology of consciousness lies in its adaptability to the laboratory setting, or, conversely, in the adaptability of the laboratory setting to various types of hypnotic contexts. However, the lack of any consensus on the status of hypnosis as an altered state of consciousness (ASC), as well as wide variability in subjects' responses to suggestion, have confounded attempts to explain the phenomenon in a rigorous, objective way (Wagstaff, 1981). Physiological and behavioral measures and verbal reports by hypnotized subjects suggest themselves as most likely to contribute to the specification of what is perhaps best thought of as "the hypothetical hypnotized state" or "the hypnotic construct." Numerous attempts have been made to determine just what the essential characteristics of hypnosis are. Pavlov (1923) defined hypnosis as partial cortical inhibition, and he also called it partial sleep, a view that has been dispelled by electroencephalographic studies (Evans, 1979). Schneck (1963) described it as a primitive psychophysiological state in which consciousness is eliminated. Kline (1958) saw it as a state characterized by a lowered criticality (less critical thinking skills involved; more accepting of data). Many other researchers have characterized hypnosis as really nothing more than hypersuggestibility.

Psychoanalysts have noted a close relationship of hypnosis with the concept of transference (Ferenczi, 1926; Gill and Brenman, 1959). It has also been considered a type of regression, but one of an atavistic type, wherein the individual returns to a mode of mental functioning that probably characterized the early development of the human species during its evolution from lower life forms. Still others have thought of hypnosis simply as a form of role playing (Watkins and Watkins, 1986). One of the more recent attempts to define the essential ingredient in hypnosis has been that of Martin T. Orne (1989). He held that the "essence" of hypnosis, that which distinguishes a truly hypnotized individual from one who is only simulating hypnosis, is the ability of a hypnotized subject to freely mix his or her perceptions of reality with those that stem from the imagination.

It would make things easier for everyone to have a specific definition for hypnosis, in order to know it when we see it or when we experience it. However, there is no simple behavioral criterion for identifying hypnosis, nor do hypnotic inductions reliably produce a hypnotic "state." Nevertheless, for our purposes let us use this good working definition of hypnosis: a psychological state or condition, induced by a ritualistic procedure, in which the subject experiences changes in perception, thinking, memory, and behavior in response to suggestions by the hypnotist (Farthing, 1992).

In posthypnotic suggestions the hypnotist suggests to subjects that after they have been aroused from hypnosis they will perform certain acts, or have certain subjective experiences, in response to specified cues. Posthypnotic suggestions are believed to be particularly important for practical applications, since they enable responsive subjects to reevaluate their experiences or modify their behavior—or at least their *perceived* experiences or behaviors. In this area, such controversial techniques as "age regression" and "retrowareness" (or "pseudoawareness") have had an enormous negative impact on perceptions of the reality of what has happened or is happening in a person's life experiences. The most damaging instances have been related to perceptions of being sexually abused and accusations of those persons perceived to have committed the abuse ("Recollections of Sex Abuse," 1993; Marino, September 1993).

All this focuses attention on two questions: just what is hypnosis, and just when is an individual hypnotized? Both research and observation indicate that many individuals apparently slip in and out of trance with little external intervention. A low score on a standard hypnotic susceptibility test does not guarantee that a subject will not slip into hypnosis in any number of circumstances.

Another factor is that hypnotized subjects apparently are very sensitive to subtle cues coming from the therapist or experimenter. Orne (1989) has called attention to the fact that hypnotists can inadvertently transmit their expectations to their subjects, who then give back to the hypnotist the desired behavior. It is not surprising that investigators often report contradictory results. Very little seems to have been done about controlling the beliefs, theories, and expectations of researchers.

Hypnosis, like a chameleon, seems to take on the beliefs and characteristics of the particular experimenter or research team by whom it is being studied. Yet most of the major controversies in the field have still not been completely and satisfactorily resolved. For example, the controversy as to whether antisocial behavior can be initiated in hypnotized individuals has raged for many years (Watkins and Watkins, 1986).

Another good example is the controversy as to whether hypnosis should be viewed as an altered state of consciousness or can be better conceptualized within a different framework. The hypnotized subject does behave in many different and apparently "nonnormal" ways, or at least is capable of doing so. He or she is more responsive to suggestion and can "remember" much more material—although a number of studies show that such "memories" may be confabulated and contaminated. In fact the verity or reality of such things as hypermnesia (total recall), age regression, and pseudo-memory is being scientifically challenged at this moment.

In a study of whether hypnosis facilitated memory of meaningful visual material that was incidentally learned, 48 undergraduate students viewed two slides, portraying different scenes, and judged how well composed they were. After hypnotic induction and guided memory instructions, or guided memory instructions alone, the students were asked to recall aspects of the scenes. The results strongly indicated that hypnosis is unlikely to facilitate memory of witnessed events (Mingay, 1986).

Memory distortion in hypnosis was shown in data from a programmatic series of studies that varied a range of conditions affecting the potential increase of recall (Sheehan, 1988). The studies used a paradigm that exposed a total of 429 students to misleading information before memory was tested and used hypnosis to test memory performance in both recognition and free recall. The results failed to demonstrate any increase in accurate memory under hypnosis; in fact, the accuracy of memory reports in hypnosis was at times significantly reduced. Also, hypnotic recall was distinctly distorted when false information was introduced after, rather than before, hypnosis.

In an investigation of hypnotic susceptibility in relation to a variety of parapsychological and anomalous feelings, beliefs, and experiences, 575 undergraduate students completed the Harvard Group Scale of Hypnotic Susceptibility, the Altered States Experiences Questionnaire, and the Cognitive Preference Questionnaire (Pekala, Kumar, and Cummings, 1992). Students with high susceptibility endorsed far more parapsychologically related items and anomalous beliefs and experiences than did students with low susceptibility. Further, a little more than 10 percent of the high susceptibles were found especially likely to report and believe in parapsychological and unusual experiences.

We can distinguish between lying and confabulation in memory reporting. "Lying" involves telling a falsehood that you know is false. "Confabulation" involves confusing fantasies with memories and *unknowingly* reporting as true memories of events that are really fantasies (Bowers, 1984). Confabulation now appears to be a common occurrence during long-term therapy, especially during hypnotic age regression, and possibly even during hypnotic eyewitness interrogation, with the "facts" actually coming from the interrogator or therapist.

The construction of memory, or confabulation, is a worrisome issue. While it is impossible to prove that a thing does *not* exist — one can only show by scientific means that something *does* exist — there is absolutely no valid evidence for the existence of long-term catastrophic memory repression. Memory is very selective. Mood, cognitive set (interpretation of environment), and associative links influence what we perceive to have happened. Our consciousness of what we believe to be "true" dictates to us what our own personal reality actually is. In large part, if we are to be contented human beings we must take control of and responsibility for how we view ourselves and others within the life we choose to lead.

Pseudomemory

In the same category as confabulation, another source of error in hypnotic recall, as well as in "standard" counseling, is pseudomemory: memories that the individual believes to be based on personal experience of an event, but which are in fact based on information learned after the event. Pseudomemories can be created when witnesses to crimes are asked leading questions during interrogation (Loftus, 1980). For example, after a physical assault on a female by an unknown male, police might ask the victim, "Did the man have brown hair and blue eyes?" Later, she might report in court that her assailant had brown hair and blue eyes, though in fact she did not see a man who fit that description.

Pseudomemories can be created by leading questions, interrogations, and therapy without any assistance from hypnosis, but hypnosis can increase the creation of pseudomemories because hypnotized subjects tend to be particularly attentive and responsive to hypnotists' communications. Pseudomemories created under hypnosis are more likely to be confidently believed by the person being questioned and to be resistant to disconfirmation through further inquiry. In fact, this scenario does occur quite frequently in judicial proceedings, with irreparable harm to the accused.

Some studies have found that hypnotized subjects are more likely than waking control subjects to reply affirmatively to false leading questions about filmed incidents they are shown. For example, hypnotized subjects were more likely to reply "yes" to the question "Did you see that green car go by?" or "Did you see the bird on top of that building?" when in fact there was no green car and no bird anywhere in the film (Putnam, 1979; Zelig and Beidleman, 1981). There is also much evidence to indicate that hypnosis increases the likelihood of pseudomemories being implanted through leading questions containing misleading information. In an elaborate experiment by Spanos, Lush, and Gwynne (1989), subjects watched a videotape of a simulated bank robbery and shooting, and later were exposed to misleading information about the robber in a videotaped newscast. Subsequently, the subjects were interrogated with leading questions about the robber ("Visualize the man's upper left arm. Do you see a tattoo?"), either with or without hypnosis; a control group was asked nonleading questions ("Describe the man"). Then the subjects tried to identify the robber in a set of photographic "mug shots." Finally, they were cross-examined by a different experimenter, who tried to get them to deny their earlier incorrect responses to interrogation questions and choices of mug shots.

Two aspects of the results were especially important: (1) Most subjects exposed to leading questions during interrogation agreed to some of them (for example, seeing a tattoo when in fact the robber had no tattoo), but hypnotized subjects were no more likely to do so than other subjects. (2) During cross-examination, most subjects retracted some of their earlier answers, but previously hypnotized persons were no more or less likely to do so than subjects not previously hypnotized. Thus, in some cases, hypnotically implanted pseudomemories are no more resistant to cross-examination than those implanted without hypnosis.

Spanos et al. concluded that during interrogation subjects responded to social pressures to answer affirmatively to leading questions. But under cross-examination a new set of social pressures was introduced, with demands for accuracy, and subjects complied by reversing some of their earlier responses. Assuming that subjects want to be both accurate and consistent, we may surmise that during cross-examination they may have felt conflict over reversing their prior responses and so did not reverse all of them, in order to save face—they did not want to admit that all of their prior responses were wrong. Spanos and McLean (1986) also concluded that social-contextual influences can affect memory reports either with or without hypnosis.

Recent studies have added to the burgeoning information concerning the potential influence of rapport on hypnotically induced pseudomemory. One study tested the effect of experimenter rapport on pseudomemory in groups of students with both high and low hypnotic susceptibility. Three sets of two-part tests were conducted, each using a hypnotist and a researcher testing pseudomemory recall. In the first test, the hypnotist criticized the students' performance, then pseudomemory was tested by the second experimenter, who also criticized the students. In the second test, the students were criticized by only one of the experimenters. In the third test, neither experimenter criticized the students. The resulting data strongly indicated a significant association between rapport with the hypnotist and pseudomemory in cued recall, the strength of pseudomemory being appreciably lowered when negative hypnotist rapport was reinforced by the person testing pseudomemory (Sheehan, Green, and Truesdale, 1992).

Fantasy

Another area of suspect memory is fantasy, which many people occasionally use to turn off the drab or irksome realities of the day. But some people, a fascinating minority, spend much of their waking lives lost in a fantasy world, leaving it only to join the common reality almost as a visitor. This type of person may, in fact, be highly susceptible to cues and instructions in leading questions pertaining to whether or they may have been abuse victims.

According to researchers, about 4 percent of people spend half or more of their waking hours absorbed in a fantasy world. These thoughts are not mere fleeting daydreams but something of a cross between a dream and a movie, in which an elaborate scenario unfolds once a theme is set. Vivid fantasies can be triggered by some chance element; the word "Egypt," for instance, can prompt a detailed mental drama about the days of the pharaohs. It does not take much of a stretch to understand the direction these people could take if multiple kinds of sexual abuse were brought into a conversation.

Research into this kind of possibility was conducted in two sessions in which independent groups of 86 and 85 college students, who had previously tested for high and low susceptibility to suggestion, respectively, answered leading questions about a video event that depicted shooting at an airport. The results showed good general effects for leading questions and a measurable level of susceptibility (Sheehan, Garnett, and Robertson, 1993). This study simply adds to the validity of other long-established conclusions of investigations which have shown, as we saw earlier in this chapter, that witnesses, victims of crimes, and others can be easily influenced by persons around them following an incident or alleged incident.

Study of the fantasy-prone is illuminating the psychological benefits as well as the pitfalls of fantasy. Recent studies of extreme fantasizers find that most are more creative and more empathetic than other people. For the most part people of this type use their extreme fantasizing ability to contribute to their own psychological well-being. However, the less functional members of this group may construct negative altered states of reality.

While there are no firm data on exactly how much time people spend in fantasy, studies of what people are doing at random times during the day have found that people's thoughts are "elsewhere" from 10 percent to 20 percent of the time. It has been stated that most daydreams are ephemeral, lasting only a few seconds. However, full-blown fantasies with complete, articulated plots are much rarer. For example, in the daydream one might consider leaving on the next plane for Paris. In the fantasy one might imagine, in detail and at length, being involved in the intrigues of some long-ago royal court ("Researchers Indicate," 1987).

For those persons at the extreme, fantasies are so compelling that they set aside special times just to immerse themselves in imaginary scenarios. Many devote an hour or two each day to fantasy; others say they have spent entire weekends alone, absorbed in intricate pretend worlds. If the ingredients of need, fear, lost parental love, imagined rejection, or any other such recipe were added to an in-depth fantasy, the consequences could be both explosive and damaging.

Recovered Memory

Explosive allegations came forth in 1993 that the leader of Chicago's archdiocese had sexually abused a young man 17 years before. These charges were based on a "recovered memory," which, despite growing skepticism in the minds of many experts in the field of human memory, is legally recognized in the courts of law in at least 22 states. In this case, 34-year-old Steven Cook filed a $10 million lawsuit against Cardinal Joseph Bernardin, charging that as a 17-year-old student at a Catholic high school in Cincinnati he had been sexually molested by the priest (*Los Angeles Times*, November 1993). Unlike most adults who say they were abused as youngsters, Cook contended that he had not deliberately hidden his experience all these years out of feelings of shame or fear or some such thing. Rather, like a growing number of people making such claims, he said he had only recently recalled the abuse while undergoing therapy. Bernardin, a highly respected Catholic prelate, vigorously denied the allegations, and Cook subsequently recanted all the charges.

This is just one in a stream of such cases in recent years. In lawsuit after lawsuit, alleged victims have based their charges on recent "recovery" of long-suppressed memory. The television talk-show circuit is overflowing with such accusations. Guests on these shows rely on a now much-disputed theory popularized by therapists, marriage counselors, and even many psychologists, which holds, basically, that the trauma of sexual abuse may cause a child to block the memory from his or her mind. The next premise is that long after the trauma actually took place, perhaps decades later, an event, or discussion with a therapist, can trigger its return. Either way, the distant past returns as a vivid memory. An array of respected psychologists have heretofore considered the theory valid and it has led to a series of court judgements on behalf of alleged victims (*San Antonio Express News*, June 1992).

However, many prominent memory experts have been debunking the notion, calling it an embarrassing mistake that is sweeping the field of human behavior. "People don't forget important things that happen to them. If you were sexually involved at age 17, you don't just forget that," says Dr. Paul McHugh, director of psychiatry at Johns Hopkins University Hospital in Baltimore (McHugh, 1993). In the essay in *American Scholar* magazine, McHugh compares this recent wave of "recovered" memory cases to the mass release of psychiatric patients in the 1970s. Both, he says, are major mistakes that simply followed the cultural fashion of the day (*San Antonio Express News*, 1993). In the 1970s, mental health professionals were swept along by the notion that psychiatric institutions were repressive places. Better to "liberate" the patients, it was felt, than to confine them in those institutions. In the 1990s, therapists have been swept along by the conviction that the sexual abuse of children is far more common than acknowledged before. Some advocates say one in three young girls is sexually abused (*Los Angeles Times*, AP, November 1993), and many therapists are now ready to believe the extraordinary numbers of adults who now say that they suffered abuse, even if they recalled it only recently.

The idea that one can totally forget a childhood trauma of some kind, and then remember it in full detail many years later (retrowareness), is now being understood by the mainstream scientific community as a myth or a hoax—something that, in reality, does not and cannot occur. It is the result of long-term therapeutic suggestion in which the ideas and "recovered" knowledge come, more often than not, from the therapist or counselor, not from the mind of the client. Although the scientific data indicate overwhelmingly that something has gone badly awry in this type of consciousness perception, alarming numbers of psychologists and psychotherapists all across the country are continuing to dredge up "long-forgotten" trauma from their patients, usually sex abuse, which may have occurred 20 to 50 years ago. ("Autistic facilitation" is another process by which "subjective" results have been shown to be externally manipulated. Here, "facilitators" use a keyboard device which purportedly allows autistic persons to exhibit their "true"—often high—intelligence. Although the procedure has failed every single test that would give it any credibility at all, it continues to be widely used in special-education settings across the United States ["Prisoners of Silence," 1993].)

If a person expected to be abused in some fashion by another person, could that expectation lead to a perception that he or she was, in fact, abused by the other person? To research this possibility, a group of 150 students was tested to determine the probability that they would expect slides of "negative" pictures—snakes, rats, bogeymen, etc.—to be paired with a shock, a tone, or nothing. Having previously been instructed that a negative picture would result in a negative action, 40 students reported a negative experience of one type or another, when actually nothing had occurred (McNally and Heatherton, 1993).

Skeptics within the scientific arena do not question the prevalence of child sexual abuse, but they strongly question the accuracy of recovered memories and the notion that childhood trauma inspires repression of its memory. Cited often as an example is the case of the children of Chowchilla, California, who were kidnapped in their school bus in 1976 and buried alive. More than 15 years after their rescue, the victims had highly detailed recollections of the entire event, and certainly did not temporarily forget any of the happenings. Also cited by many in the scientific community are stories of Holocaust survivors, who were rounded up as children, many decades later remembering their experiences in great detail. The problem with great trauma is *over-remembering*—the victims cannot get the memories out of their heads even if they want to.

Critics have also pointed to the large number of therapists who are eager to believe that their troubled clients most likely suffered a sexual trauma. If that is so, the victims' recovery may well require them to distill the memory of this trauma and to confront the perpetrators; but some medical experts fear that these "memories" are being created. At its 1993 meeting, the American Medical Association passed a resolution condemning the misuse of hypnosis and other techniques in memory enhancement. No experiments have demonstrated at any valid level that memories can be repressed and then reliably recovered. While a patient's reports of dreams and flashbacks can sometimes prove useful in therapy, not a single credible study has shown that these visions are the least bit authentic (*San Antonio Express-News*, 1993).

Age Regression

Part of the thesis of this book is that through an understanding of consciousness and several of its altered states we can become aware that at least two of these states—hypnosis and "deep" therapy—can cause the construction of major errors in "reality." As mentioned previously, age regression and post-traumatic memory retrieval, which coalesce in the notion that long-forgotten memories of childhood abuse can be brought forth decades after the event, are highly suspect as far as actual fact is concerned.

The concept of psychological regression is an important one for the fields of developmental and clinical psychology. Many have cited the dramatic and seemingly compelling childlike performances of hypnotically age-regressed individuals as evidence that, under some circumstances, it is possible for an individual to return to an earlier developmental stage of psychological functioning.

A review of more than 100 empirical studies over 60 years found no convincing evidence that early developmental psychological structures are reinstated, in the form of age-regression "memories," during hypnosis. However, evidence was found that hypnosis enables persons to elicit more imagistic, primary process (the simple *idea* of being hypnotized results in pretension and/or imitation), affect-laden material (coming up with what you think you are *supposed* to come up with). It was suggested that the core assumptions underlying the concept of temporal regression are correlationally weak and should be reexamined (Nash, 1988).

In a study at Ohio University (Lynn, Milano, and Weekes, 1992) nine hypnotizable university students and eight simulating hypnosis were age-regressed to the previous week's hypnosis session and received the suggestion that they had heard a phone ring during the earlier session (no phone actually rang). In response to open-ended questions, no students indicated that a real phone actually rang. In response to a forced-choice question, slightly more than 22 percent of the hypnotizable and 25 percent of the simulating students indicated that the suggested phone ring was an actual event. The researchers suggested that when the event that is the subject of a pseudomemory suggestion is *publicly verifiable*, the pseudomemory rate is very low.

In an experiment at Monmouth College in West Long Branch, New Jersey (Coram and Hafner, 1988), 40 college students who had scored high or low on a test of hypnotic susceptibility were studied to compare the content of early recollections obtained while in the hypnotic state. Recollections of early development were also obtained from the students during a normal waking state. Accuracy of recall, qualitative changes, and effects on productivity of recall versus accurate recall were examined. The final data suggested that the content of early recollections changed following a hypnotic induction procedure and that these changes may have been driven by the students' a priori beliefs, by experimenter behavior, and by the desire to reduce anxiety. Thus, the validity of early recollections under hypnosis remains very questionable.

The power of wanting to believe something creates a vested interest in regarding it as true even when all indications are that it is not. Scientists who try to put forth the facts to make the public aware of what actually is the case will be castigated, chastised, and virtually "tarred and feathered." An article in the American Counseling Association publication the *Guidepost* in September 1993 (Marino) gave an account of a number of families that had been ruined by child molestation charges based on "retrieved" memory, only to find out later that the charges were not based in fact at all. The very next issue of the *Guidepost* (Morrissey, October 1993) carried a number of letters to the editor stating how terrible it was that such an article could be written. One even went so far as to allude to the possibility that the author of the article might have a less than "acceptable attitude toward child sexual molestation"! The letters were not from the general public; these nasty accusatory comments came from licensed mental health providers. And examples of this type of reaction are quite numerous.

It cannot be stated too strongly that the whole idea of "reconstructing" memories of abuse is quite suspect. An important part of therapy with survivors of abuse is to help put the parts of what happened back together again from shattered bits and pieces of potential recall. It should be obvious how subjective a process this is. Any suggestion by the interviewer will have a significant effect on all possible responses of the abused person. In clinical psychology it is "taught" that the client's history of intrusive symptoms provides a way to anticipate the nature of the trauma, even when no memory of any actual event really exists.

Indications are that simply thinking about a particular topic can enhance the believability of whatever is being thought about (Feltz and Landers, 1983). Consequently, it would not take a large leap of logic to understand that talking about sexual abuse, for example, with a client who has no memory of any such thing can greatly influence what that person might later begin to think had actually happened.

According to frequent reports by the American Psychological Association, about one in every three U.S. women will be physically assaulted by a male partner during her lifetime ("One Woman in Three," 1994). These reports are summaries of current scientific findings on violence of all kinds, against women, children, and men. It must be stated again that no one, including myself, seriously believes there is not an alarming amount of different kinds of abuse going on all over the world. However, that is all the more reason to be extremely discriminating when making such charges.

To sum up, in scientific circles the evidence is overwhelming concerning the lack of credible data to indicate that any such thing as "retrowareness" or "recovered memory" exists at all in any form. In fact, the evidence is quite strong to the contrary, that is to say, that the "memory" comes from other persons (counselors, therapists, police authorities, religious figures, child protection officers, etc.), all of whom have some vested interest in the "recovered memory" syndrome. Such an interest does not necessarily have malice attached to it. Actually, in the great majority of cases there is probably no intent to harm others or gain personal benefit. However, that is exactly what seems to be the result in a large number of cases. A very profitable industry has developed from claims of being able to retrieve memory, and a multitude of human lives have been ruined by those induced "memories."

CHAPTER 5

Counseling Psychology

In this chapter we will examine counseling, or "talk therapy," in general, and its most important branch, family-systems therapy, in particular. We will consider the recent criticisms of this approach and the evidence that supports its effectiveness; in particular, we will look at approaches to research that focus on the therapeutic process and on the outcomes of therapy. Two related areas—the technique of team therapy and influences on the development of psychologists' theoretical orientations—will also be discussed.

Family-Systems Therapy

> I evaluate family therapy as a rather sad sack relying for its status largely on assertion, self-congratulation, guruism and denigration of alternatives. Like psychoanalysis, family therapy resembles a religion rather than a proper professional endeavour [Werry, 1989, p. 377–382].

After being accepted by the professional community comparatively quickly during the last two or three decades, there seems to now be developing a rather wide range of criticism toward family therapy, and counseling psychology in general, as a legitimate therapeutic undertaking. The obvious questions to ask are: What, basically, is counseling therapy? Is it useful? Is it harmful? Is there any valid research? If so, what does it say? Who is right? Is anyone right? Is anyone wrong?

Pinning down the exact starting point of family psychotherapy is somewhat difficult to do. However, the consensus seems to be that serious methodology formulations began shortly after World War II (Goldenberg and Goldenberg, 1985). This was the epoch in counseling when practitioners began to look at the family's role in the causation and continuation of psychological dysfunction in one or more individual members of a family. In the massive reunification of families after the war, the comparatively quick "remaking" of the family structure brought about a multitude of social, interpersonal, and cultural problems.

At the same time that psychological intervention was becoming a more acceptable way for people to deal with emotional stress, the "rightness" of the idea of working with the complete family rather than the individual was also gaining considerable ground. Also, whereas in the past psychiatrists had held a virtual monopoly in the treatment of mental health, the field was allowing access to a much broader spectrum of practitioners: marriage counselors, psychotherapists, pastoral counselors, and social workers.

The basic idea behind family therapy is simply that no individual lives in a vacuum. A family is a social system, one that has developed a specific set of rules and regulations. There are certain recognizable forms of communication and negotiation. Each part of this system is bound together with the other parts by very powerful and emotional attachments. What any one part of the system does may have consequences for any or all of the other members of the system.

As a total system, a family makes continuous attempts to organize itself into a functioning group. Members normally share a common household and try to engage in behavior that is cooperative and beneficial to the entire system. Even after children grow up and leave the initial home structure, the family influence continues and is passed on to subsequent generations. The family system is generally distinguished from all other social combinations by the strength and character of its loyalty, affection, and durability (Brown, 1986). However, the basic structure is the same as in any social system. Also, its composition can include nuclear families, stepfamilies, single-parent families, common-law families, and extended families.

Over the past three decades or so, the following concept of family therapy has emerged: An individual who exhibits socially unacceptable or dysfunctional behavior (depression, alcoholism, drugs, sexual problems, anxieties, etc.) may simply be showing the manifestations of a family (system) that has developed "flaws" in its normal structure. Consequently, the reasons for and nature of the individual's dysfunction cannot possibly be made clear through the study of that one person by him or herself (Goldenberg and Goldenberg, 1985). It would thus seem obvious and proper that understanding such a situation could only be accomplished within the context of the complete family social system.

Probably the most influential theoretical approach to family counseling therapy is "structural" therapy. The term basically refers to the concept of focusing on the active and organized wholeness of the system (Brown, 1986). Important emphasis is placed on when, how, and to whom family members currently relate, in order to understand the family structure and then to change it into a more positive one. The family structure includes not only the totality of the main system itself but a specific compilation of subsystems as well. These subsystems pertain to the separate family domains—the parents' and the children's—and to how the different family members relate: children to parents, father to children, and children to mother, and so on. How the "consciousness" of each individual views the other members of the structure is highly important.

Each of the multiplicity of subsystems within the family structure has individual and, for the most part, well understood "boundaries." There is a tendency for autonomy and permeability—both of which are proper and needed—to balance out within and between the subsystems. When the leveling effects of systemic communication breaks down, the positive circularity of the situation begins to whirl itself apart.

Overall, a "family system" is defined as people maintaining a specified position that is in constant reciprocal interaction. Another definition could be: A family consists of those members within the construct maintaining a state of continually occurring reciprocal influence (Ackerman, 1984). These definitions could also include any and all groups committed to permanent relationships. What is basically required is that the general relationship of the members of a "family" must be known, in addition to the characteristics of the individuals themselves.

Family therapy has evolved from the belief that the actions and interactions of individual members, as they relate to each other and to the whole, determine the health or dysfunction of the individuals and the system. Broken down into further subparts: An action has strength and direction and can be perceived visually, aurally, and kinesthetically (Ackerman, 1984). When the action is directed at a relationship, it may be followed by interaction, which is a "facilitating" action, or by less action, which is termed an "interruption." These interactions constitute a continuum within the system and result, depending on whether they are positive or negative, in well-being or the lack thereof for the individual or the system. Basically, it is the job of the family psychotherapist to realign and reframe these relationships from a negative spiral to a positive circularity.

Criticisms of Family Therapy

"The declining role of religion in guiding people's way of explaining their personal and interpersonal problems has led to the wide acceptance of psychological attributions" (Furman and Tapani, 1989, pp. 33–38). In an article appearing in *Family Systems Medicine*, the authors put forth the complaint that the pervasive availability through the mass media of information about common psychological attributions, further spread by word of mouth, has adverse effects on society at large. The thought is that attributing family pathology directly to specific "problems" in life tends to discourage people from solving their own difficulties. To reverse the idiom, life begins to imitate art—in this case, television. Our conscious perception of what is "real" changes in accordance with what we are *taught* is real.

The same article goes on to state that this type of attitude will possibly lead to a society in which the numbers of psycho-professionals grow and help is sought from them by people who have "minor" problems. Some of the many adverse effects resulting from a growing tendency to depend on other people to solve one's problems could include guilt, shame, a belief that one is "mentally ill," and the casting of blame—parents blaming children and children blaming parents. The article ends by stating that serious scientific attention and study needs to be given to the negative possibilities of family therapy.

In psychotherapy, a major problem arises on the topic of the "family" itself (Saraceno, 1990). This criticism relates to a difficulty of definition. What seems to be at issue is to what extent it is possible to talk of the family system as a subject possessed of its own intentionality, interests, rationality, and needs, *distinct* from those of its individual members. Saraceno's conclusion is that it is probably a good idea to realize that the "family," as a specific social subject for treatment, should be discussed only with extreme caution. The fear is that this is not always the case.

In an article in the *Journal of Family Therapy* in 1989, provocatively titled "Family Therapy—Professional Endeavour or Successful Religion?" John S. Werry, a psychiatrist, blasted the total concept of family therapy with a rather scathing critique and review: "Family therapy should be judged by its scientific merit, not such things as formal logic, intuition and experience. If it was it would fail miserably" (pp. 377–382). Werry compares much of the methodology of family therapy to such practices of an earlier era as lobotomies, bleeding, and purging. Looking back over the past thirty years, he says, of the four major therapies—pharmacotherapy, behavior therapy, psychoanalysis, and family therapy—the least effective (maybe even harmful) is family-systems therapy. He goes on to say family therapy has many of the hallmarks of a religion, with several competing sects led by feuding charismatic prophets. This attitude, he goes on, can be related to all counseling psychology. At the same time, it has few of the attributes of a true professional endeavour rooted in scientific ethics and skepticism. Werry ends by stating that until family therapy allows itself to be tested using scientific methodology, the major question remains, should it be supported at all?

In a somewhat surprising turn of events, in the same issue as Dr. Werry's, there was another critical slap at family therapy, this one from the editor of the magazine, Bryan Lask. Lask (1989) writes about an International Family Therapy Conference he had recently attended. As he was listening to a "very important person's" presentation, his mind began to wander into kind of a fairy-tale mode. Lask then tells the story of a very sad and lonely family therapist. Her name was Aft (average family therapist). She was feeling bad because all of her colleagues were away at a conference and she was left alone to take care of the clinic. She began to have a dream that she was visited by the patron saint of family therapists, whose name was Virginia.

To make a long (and fairly humorous) story shorter, Saint Virginia took Aft's hand and they were transported through the night to this very important family conference. Aft found herself listening to a very important-looking person. She felt stupid because she wasn't quite sure what his message was. "The new paradigm allows us to have a dialogic on radical constructivism," he was saying. She listened harder. "Marriage is a conversation." That sounded good, but what did it mean? "Sex and time are metaphors, even metaphors are metaphors. . . . If a marriage is a conversation, sex is talking dirty." Aft didn't really get any of this. When she woke up, she discovered that the worst thing that could ever happen to a family therapist had happened to her: she had turned into a *linear thinker!* Even though Lask's story is told in a humorous vein, it provides a good example of the distortion of some of the subsets of consciousness, such as internal knowledge, direct awareness, and personal unity.

A family therapist who sees an entire family in therapy sets him- or herself up as an arbiter of human values, according to Jeffrey M. Masson in his book *Against Therapy* (1988). By the definition of the concept, a family therapist sees "sick" families; the therapist is the one who defines what the sickness is. There is a tendency to blame the victims of actions such as family violence. Masson goes on to say that according to family therapy theory, the wife or child of an abusive man may have been an "unwitting collaborator." In addition, within family therapy a large number of culturally sanctioned assumptions are brought into play as if they were brand-new insights. As it turns out, Masson says, these assumptions are rarely more than prejudices. Many times individuals within a family structure are labeled in a positive or negative manner by the therapist, but these labels have no validity to them at all; they are nothing more than personal value judgements by the therapist. Playing the great and wise guru is endemic among family therapists. The therapist firmly believes that he or she knows best in all cases and normally puts up no pretense to the contrary.

Rebuttal

Now, what historical and contemporary indications are there that family-systems therapy works? First, before one can know if a particular methodology can be and is successful, one must know the *goals* of that methodology. If the goals are reached, the method works.

There is, of course, a multitude of goals in family therapy, virtually as many as there are complaints or problems. But the central goal of systemic therapy would seem to be making the system work both for its individual members and as a unit. This objective seems to be somewhat contradictory, placing the autonomy and competence of individual members in competition with "healthy" family interactions (L'Abate, Ganahl, and Hansen, 1986). But, as mentioned earlier, it relates to the realization of familial and individual balance. An immediate goal would be to obtain symptomatic relief, with long-term goals aimed at improved intrafamilial communication.

In the most direct sense, all goals would pertain to making a "problem" not a problem any longer. Something is only a problem if it is *perceived* as such by one or more members of the family. If that particular point of view can be changed, then "health" has been restored and all goals have been met. In this view, the family should be allowed to use its own criteria to construct their systemic goals, with the therapist in the role of facilitator (Bell, 1975). This would relate directly to human consciousness and its perception of "positive" goals.

In a more recent evolution of the family therapy process, a methodology known as "solution therapy" has come to the fore. Its alignment with the norms of standard family counseling is still quite strong; however, there are some specific differences. Put simply, it is a method that relates to and depends upon peoples' competence and strengths rather than deficiencies and weaknesses (O'Hanlon and Weiner-Davis, 1989). There are three basic goals: Change the *doing* of whatever is perceived as being a problem, change how that situation is *viewed*, and evoke natural resources and strengths to bring about *solutions* to what is thought of as the problem.

Research

In this section we will examine two approaches to research into systems therapy: *process* research and *outcome* research, that is, evaluation of therapy based on research into either the therapeutic process itself or the ultimate outcome of that therapy. We will start with the former.

Raymond Corsini and Danny Wedding (1989) report a study of individual casework in the field of marital counseling which compared single-client sessions with conjoint ones, using the process notes of the therapist. The weakness in the study, the authors concluded, was that for some reason the process notes did not always reflect what occurred during the sessions.

In another study (Sahiro and Budman, 1973), the emphasis shifted from the therapist to the family and seemed to show that what the therapist does or does not do is of high import in determining the continuation or termination of the family treatment. These findings also match the theoretical constructs of several other theorists in the field (Haley, 1980). Further studies using direct observation have also been used in process research (e.g., Williams 1989). One such study compared real responses in therapy and simulated ones. The relationship between the responses of family therapy trainees and the outcome of therapy for families they had treated were also considered. However, Corsini and Wedding (1989) say the results were mixed. They also indicate that one of the main weaknesses in this study was having to rely on the response of the therapist.

The area of process and research dealing with it still seem to be in the early developmental stages (Corsini and Wedding, 1989). The reason seems to be that it is inherently difficult to develop a valid research instrument for this topic. Systems therapy necessarily involves a number of people, and this means that a large number of variables have to be controlled. A related problem might have to do with the inability to replicate exact cases. However, that said, family therapy process does show numerous signs of heading in a direction that will extend its already demonstrated practicality.

At bottom, all communication results in therapeutic intervention of one kind or another; therefore, the fact that, at this time, there are not one or two or three specific and "correct" process tracks to follow does not directly affect the workability of the approach.

Outcome research is a more developed area than process research. This is due largely to the work of Alan Gurman and Andrew Raxin (1987). Gurman and Raxin reached 19 specific conclusions pertaining to family therapy and its outcome. Some of the most relevant ones are:

Nonbehavioral marital therapy is of benefit in about two-thirds of the cases.

Therapy with both spouses is more effective.

Length of treatment does not correlate with effectiveness.

At times family therapy makes relationships worse.

Individual therapy is ineffective with marital problems.

Conjoint therapy is effective.

The severity of a problem is not a determining factor in the outcome.

Gurman and Raxin also cite the therapies they believe have been most effective: Minuchin's work with psychosomatic families (structural), Stanton and Todd's (1979) work with drug addicted families (structural), and operantly oriented behavior therapy aimed at changing intrafamilial childhood behaviors.

Other case studies focusing on problem description and outcome include investigations of family therapy concentrating on child conduct disorders. The main formulation for treatment here is called "parent management training," that is, training of the parents by the therapist. The technique is based on the general view that conduct problems are inadvertently developed and sustained in the home by maladaptive child-parent interactions and that altering these interaction patterns can decrease the child's antisocial behavior.

Many therapeutic interactions include a procedure that is known as "perturbing the system"—introducing a change into the family structure and thus reframing it. Several studies have revealed marked positive changes over the course of treatment and followups one year later showed that gains are often maintained (Williams and Spitzer, 1983).

There was, however, a major criticism of the results of these studies, cited by Williams and Spitzer (1983), which I found amusing. Dr. Donald Klein of the New York State Psychiatric Institute stated at the annual meeting of the American Psychopathological Association in 1983 that in evaluations of the therapy, the "parents and the teachers are the ones who have rated the biggest effects. This questions what you are finding. There is a need for an independent evaluator" (Barrel, May 1985). If I understand Dr. Klein correctly, he is saying that just because the parents say the child is no longer a problem and the teachers say the child is no longer a problem, and the child does not identify a problem, the child still may *actually* have a problem.

Taken together, these studies give a clear and concise indication that systems therapy (counseling psychology) has the power to produce change. It is not clear exactly *how* this is accomplished or *why* one approach seems to be more or less effective than another. It would seem to have as much to do with the perceptions of both therapist and patients as with any planned methodology. Personal, conscious organization of therapeutic information makes virtually all the difference in whether the results of psychotherapy encounters conclude positively or negatively.

External Reality

Does the "kind" of person a client is—his or her religion, language, culture, skin color—make a difference in therapy, dictate the type of counseling methodology to be used, or necessitate specific background and training of the therapist? While there are some who still say no, at least not to any great extent, a number of others practicing in the field now say an important ingredient in therapy may have been overlooked for some time. Many now believe that to "fix" the internal workings of a family one must be aware of and work within the context of the *external reality* of that family.

In an article in the *Journal of Family Therapy* (1990), Charles O'Brian, a black family therapist, states that of all the differences in peoples of the world, it is color which most sets them apart and color which most binds them together. He goes on to say that other differences, such as language, religion, and culture, are important to consider in family therapy. But the most important by far in determining one's external reality, he insists, is the color of one's skin.

Doman Lum (1986) states in reference to the "American perspective" that the common experiences of racism, discrimination, and segregation bind people of color together and contrast with the experience of white Americans. Salvador Minuchin (1984), acknowledging omissions in an earlier work, admits, "I drew boundaries that separated the family from its context. In staking my territory and proclaiming expertise on the interior of the family reality, I was declaring ignorance about other aspects of the family reality."

The basic premise of this viewpoint is that the boundary between family and society is permeable; at this boundary there is actually a meshing of the two. The cases that would show this in the most extreme and tangible ways relate to severely disadvantaged families. Much of the time of these people is taken up with the daily task of survival. The external system defines so much of their lives that it seems quite ludicrous for the therapist to ignore it, even in part.

Recognizing that racism is part of the fabric of both American and British society, O'Brian (1990) makes a short list of certain facts he believes therapists should be aware of:

1. Black children are more likely to be received into care than white children.

2. Compulsory admissions to psychiatric hospitals are more frequently used with black people than with white people.
3. Black offenders are less likely to be recommended for probation and are more likely to receive custodial sentences.
4. Black people have a much higher representation in areas of poor housing.
5. The educational system severely disadvantages black children.

In closing, O'Brian quotes a passage from Minuchin (1984), whom he identifies as an influential family and systems theorist, that might offer some clues on how to proceed in rectifying what O'Brian sees as a major problem that lies in the way of successful intervention: "Social systems like families tend to maintain their organization unchanged. But since they are open systems, they also respond to inputs by restructuring. The challenge then is how to become an irritant for positive change" (p. 22).

What became quite clear to me during the investigation which resulted in this book, however, is that over the past several decades the "irritant" has resulted in massive *negative* change within both social systems and families.

An article by M. Mydell, titled "Understanding Arabs," in the *Journal of Cross-Cultural Psychology* (1990), indicates similar thinking about the importance of external reality when working in family therapy. The author observes that Islam remains the key to their understanding for Arabs, who are characterized as religious, fatalistic, generous, humanitarian, and loyal, as well as emotional and ambivalent. This, Mydell says, would seem to have great impact on how to treat them therapeutically.

A *Handbook for Developing Multicultural Awareness*, by Paul Pedersen (1990), gives multiple indications that the external environment of individuals and families greatly affects counseling and development within the systemic structure. For example, he includes a model of multicultural counselor training called the Triad Model. Counseling in this context is conceived in terms of three simultaneous dialogues: the dialogue between the counselor and the client, the counselor's internal dialogue, and the client's internal dialogue.

The April 1990 issue of the *Journal of Consulting and Clinical Psychology* contains an article titled "An 11-Year Analysis of Black

Students' Experience of Problems and Use of Services" (June and Curry, 1990) The gist of this article is that such issues as finances, academic adjustment, and living conditions have crucial implications in the area of counseling of black students. The authors also provide statistics showing that use of counseling services may be directly related to the social, financial, cultural, and geographic background of the students' families.

A large amount of recent information seems to point to the possibility that environment does have an important impact on family therapy methodology and training. There is some evidence (Teplin, 1990) that even very short-term incarceration in jail may alter the way such persons should be counseled in later life. Teplin further notes, as a positive movement, that studies in this area are taking place, and believes much more is needed and would be welcomed.

Team Therapy

Viewing and participating in team counseling sessions over the years has led me to a number of varied thoughts, questions, and ideas. At this point, these thoughts are mostly in the form of inquiries and postulations that attempt to formulate the basis for further learning, and this section is based on these unfinished musings. What is obvious to one person may not be obvious to another. In fact, there are many people who make a living as "experts" on the obvious; therefore, there must be a need for it.

Many years of trial-and-error experience have gone into the methodology used in these counseling sessions. Following the exact "track" or "outline" of the sessions would seem to me to be as good a way as any of understanding them. Consequently, I have narrowed my scope in this section to focus mainly on the positive and negative aspects of *how* to get from one "signpost" of team counseling to another.

As a member of many therapy teams, I have observed that the following seems to be the basic formula or methodology used: First the two (or sometimes more) counselors interview the potential client in an attempt to determine what the problem is and to obtain as much background information as is necessary at that time. The interview is typically held in a room with a one-way mirror through which part of the team can observe unseen. Then the therapists meet in a brief session to exchange information and ideas before the actual counseling encounter begins. During the first interaction with the client, the team attempts to put the person at ease as much as possible. They talk about such things as background, family, job, and friends. They may get specific about the problem at hand and its roots, or they may not during this initial encounter. There is a definite beginning, middle, and close to this session as well as to the few as 5 or as many as 100 that follow.

It seems to me that in this kind of therapy situation it is very important that the counselors be closely in tune with each other's thinking and the exact pathway they are going to take during the session. The encounter must also seem as natural and informal as possible. The counselors certainly should try very hard not to make it obvious that they are searching for the next question to ask; even more important, they must not, through inattention, ask a question that has already been answered.

One of the things that struck me during team sessions was the importance of the therapists' ability to pay attention. When therapists were not able to, part of the reason for it was surely that they were trying very hard to remember what to do or say next. This, of course, is completely normal when a student is going through the learning process, but is not acceptable in a seasoned professional. The patients in these situations are real people with very real problems. I wonder if there may be another way for the teams to become more polished when working with actual cases. If not, maybe the team concept should be rethought.

There also seems to be a great deal of evading and avoiding the issues at hand on the part of the therapists. In the sessions I attended, I rarely heard anyone ask, "What is the problem?" or "What do you think the reasons for the problem are?" or "How do you think this problem can be solved?" or "What steps can you take to make things better?" The attitude seemed to be that a certain amount of time had to be filled, so we did not want to ask any hard and specific questions for fear the answers might sum it up and leave us with nothing else to do.

Team therapy is not unlike a sales presentation or a marketing program. To me, that is not necessarily a bad thing, but it certainly has the potential to be so. One uses the same tools—basically, leading clients in the direction you want them to go—for different reasons and with different goals. You want them to adopt more positive ways of perceiving themselves and others.

My concerns about team therapy, at this point, tend to focus on four basic areas: The lack of specific questioning; the tendency to make much too much out of subtle responses from the patient; the lack of sufficient direction; and the real danger that team therapy can fall into the trap of becoming a kind of vaudevillian side show in which the team is the "act" and the patient is simply the audience.

The "Very Smart Person" Syndrome

There is a phenomenon that is said to occur in many graduate psychology training programs. It is called the "very smart person" syndrome (Lask, 1989). This refers to the tendency of graduate psychology students to relate to their most influential professors or teachers as gurus. The observation of this phenomenon has led to accusations, as noted earlier, that some theories within the arena of counseling psychology, such as family therapy, might be more closely aligned with religion than with psychotherapy (Werry, 1989).

This phenomenon should be of no small interest to graduate students. An appreciation of it may allow them to have some understanding of the degree to which they may be methodologically "programmed" in the practice of their future careers. It should be equally important for teaching professors as well as practicing psychologists to be aware of the strength and lasting impact their influence may — or may not — have on the continuing growth and direction of the field as a whole.

To determine the degree of theoretical influence that graduate students perceive themselves to be receiving while involved in their graduate training, I conducted an empirical study. I also sought to determine the degree to which perceived theoretical influence obtained during graduate training continued to apply among practicing psychologists after working in the field for five years or more. The final step in my study was to compare the two group results so as to differentiate between perceived future influence and actual influence in professional practice.

A review of the literature revealed a number of related studies pertaining to the arena of training and influence as a whole. A survey of orientations of professional psychologists in clinical practice and their former professors (Sammons and Gravitz, 1990) suggested a significant relation between educators' attempts to influence students and students' perceptions of such attempts. However, that study showed only moderate correlation between educators and students in reference to theoretical orientation and perceptions thereof. Similar studies also concluded that counseling psychologists may have possibly been influenced by their former professors (Smith, 1982).

While research has been done in peripheral regions of the same topical boundaries—for example, on the potential influence on graduate training of previous employment experiences (Feis, Mavis, Weth, and Davidson, 1990), on the impact of personal skills, competencies, and interests before and during graduate training on professional application (Watkins, Schneider, Manus, and Hunton-Shoup, 1990), and on the possible influence of graduate training on the current renewed interest in eclecticism as a therapeutic methodology (Jensen, Bergin, and Greaves, 1990)—prior to my study there had been no attempts to assess the perceived influence of psychology professors' theoretical orientations on their students, either during graduate training or after five or more years of practice.

I based my study on the hypothesis that graduate students of psychology perceive that they are being theoretically influenced more strongly and lastingly than they actually are. It was predicted that this would be shown if the theoretical orientations of practicing professionals were found *not* to have been very highly influenced by their graduate training. Thus, perceived future influence would be shown as much higher than actual influence.

Ninety-two graduate psychology students and 30 practicing and teaching psychologists responded to self-explanatory questionnaires using a Likert (attitude) scale. Both sets of questionnaires were identical except in tense: questions for graduate students used the term "will influence," while those for professors used the term "continues to influence." Responses rated six degrees of influence: (1) No influence; (2) very little influence; (3) more than a little influence; (4) strong influence; (5) very strong influence; (6) total influence.

The results seemed to indicate that graduate students in the field of psychology are, in fact, influenced to a significant degree by their instructors, especially by whomever they consider their "favorite" professor. However, it is probably safe to say the data also showed that five to ten years into their actual practice, psychologists do not continue to be as strongly influenced as they were just after completion of graduate school. Nevertheless, this does seem to be an area of training which warrants close scrutiny, lest "manipulation" of erroneous points of view be passed down through multiple generations of psychotherapists.

It would seem to me that one of the most influential tools in therapy is an innate sympathy for those you are counseling—and I am *not* talking about "conspicuous compassion." Going around telling everyone how "sensitive" you are does not make it true; in fact, if anything, it is fairly irritating. What I am talking about is a genuine caring personality. If that is not part of a counselor's character repertoire, the client in need of serious emotional help will know it right away and credibility will be completely lost.

A lot of the criticisms of various therapeutic approaches may simply be matters of modality preference—transactional versus existential, Adlerian versus psychodrama, Gestalt versus rational-emotive, and so forth. My own preference leans toward William Glasser and the Reality Therapy approach. "The therapist has the task of teaching his patients to acquire the ability to fulfill their needs and to do so in a way that does not deprive others of the ability to fulfill their needs" (Glasser, 1965, p. 18).

This seems to be a matter of responsibility. Many of the problems I have heard people talking about in therapy sessions are comparatively common. They are the kind of thing that life is all about. That is not to say they are not big problems to the people concerned, or that they do not need or cannot use emotional support; they certainly do and can. What it does mean, in my opinion, is that they need to be given strong direction when receiving counseling. They need to be shown that they do have worth and abilities and that they can help themselves to become happier, healthier human beings.

Therapists, counselors, psychologists, and psychiatrists aside, it is the patient who will have to overcome whatever problems he or she is dealing with, and they will have to do it basically alone. The only thing the second party can do, whoever that might be, is to teach that kind of responsibility. I know that this is not the only way of thinking about the problem, but it is my way of thinking about it and, in doing so, of believing in the system.

My thoughts are more about the content of the package, so to speak, than about the package itself. I think the container—that guide which puts boundaries, limits, and signposts on the tangible construction of psychotherapy—is somewhat tried and true and, at least for present purposes, workable. However, it is what goes on inside the package—the container—in my opinion, that has more to do with its success or failure than anything else. The proper content—actions and interactions through different kinds of communication between therapist and patient—will many times be successful without any professional packaging at all. At the same time, the greatest packaging in the world is just worthless wrapping paper without the necessary content—the ability to relate to the patient in a completely sympathetic manner while giving direction along the way.

I do not believe there is any doubt that some of the critical arrows shot at family therapy and counseling psychology in general have hit right on target. However, those who believe there is much of value to be found within therapeutic communication, interaction, and intervention should keep a constant vigil against getting trapped in the master-therapist-guru syndrome. There may be definite power, influence, and worth in family psychotherapy. It is a complex and sophisticated way of working with human life and its problems. But one has only to hear the whispered "oohs" and "aahs" that permeate a crowd of young practitioners or graduate students listening to the latest "very smart person" to realize that the human species seems to have a strong desire, maybe even a need, to believe the emperor really *does* have clothes.

CHAPTER 6

Negative Altered States

Human beings respond in a somewhat predictable way to the environment (reality) in which they live. If the foundation of those surroundings is blurred, continually changing, lacking dependability, or only "virtually" real (as in television), then these human beings will exist in a state of constant tension and anxiety. Their grasp on what is real will be considerably weakened and they will respond—act and react—to perceived reality. Their "personal unity" will be relegated to a state of disarray. This will result in a seminal crack in the basic structure of what, over only the past few thousand years, has become formulated as acceptable social behavior. The reason for this is that people of all social strata respond in the way they have been *taught* to respond, but now the way in which their consciousness perceives their environment has been changed by massive amounts of erroneous information input.

The social and philosophical issues discussed in this chapter have great bearing on human awareness (consciousness). They add important information about the current states of negative realities pointed to throughout this book, and contribute to the potential for creating a multiplicity of positive states while there is still the will to do so.

Social Psychology

In this section we will explore the contributions of social psychology to the understanding of some of these negative and positive states. The topics covered include social influence and norms, aggression, helping behavior, loneliness, and love.

What causes people to do certain things? In a general way, *conformity* comes about when what one believes or how one acts is changed as the result of pressure to be like "the rest," or possibly as the result of actually wanting to be like the group. The individual may or may not believe as the group does; coercion could be the reason for the change in behavior. *Informational social influence* causes a person to accept a group's opinion of the way things really are; there is no discrepancy between the individual's beliefs and the group's. *Normative social influence* is pressure to believe in a particular idea or position that one does not actually believe in; even if one does give in to the pressure and behaves like the group, it is against one's true will.

Social norms are standards of behavior or rules that groups and individuals are expected to obey; these concern such matters as proper dress, hair length, manners, actions, and so forth. The norms may apply to society as a whole or just to a small group of co-workers or associates or friends. Norms develop in order to provide stability and continuity for society and a "frame of reference" for the individual.

In a classic study, Muzafer Sherif (1936) put individuals and groups of people in a dark room with only one small light, which appeared to move in different directions around the room. The effect known as autokinetics caused the illusion of movement, though the light really did not move. When there was only one person in the room at a time, the degrees of movement reported varied greatly. However, the reports of movement were very similar when the light was seen by a group; there seemed to be a process of consensus. It took longer for the persons who had previously viewed the light by themselves to come around to the group's way of thinking, but they did. This is considered an "informational influence" study because there was actual "private acceptance." Something was not true, but was believed to be true.

In a study by Henri Tajfel (1982) a *minimal group situation* was created, in which small groups of individuals were grouped together for meaningless or superficial reasons (actually, for no real reason), to see if they would be competitive against other groups just because they *were* other groups. The study found that groups *did* tend to band together against other groups just because of the group identification. "Social categorization" itself is enough reason to discriminate against the group of "others." The massive proliferation of gangs over the past 20 years is one result of such a mind-set, as are the much larger and more dangerous examples of ethnicity against ethnicity and country against country.

Social psychologists have somewhat differing definitions of *aggression*. Robert Baron (1977) says that any behavior which is meant to harm another person who does not want to be harmed is aggression. Others (e.g., Berkowitz, 1984) distinguish between "behavioral" aggression and "emotional" aggression. Although the idea is now losing ground, many scientists had previously thought aggression to be totally natural. The major argument against the "instinctual" theory says that it is an example of circular reasoning: aggression is found everywhere throughout history; the aggressive society of humans must be the result of aggressive instinct; as proof of this, instinct theorists point to the prevalence of aggression everywhere.

The three social psychological theories of aggression have more to do with *learned behavior*. *Drive theory* sees external events as causing violence; *social learning theory* says behavior is modeled on other people's actions; *individual difference theory* posits that you might hurt someone just because they are not like you.

Certain terms often come up in psychological discussions of violence on television and in the movies. *Disinhibition* refers to people thinking it is all right to engage in aggressive behavior if the mass media contain the message that such acts are justified or even proper under certain conditions (*Rambo* and *Dirty Harry* are examples. *Activation of aggressive response tendencies* has to do with the "readiness" of the viewer to be aggressive in response to "cues" from television. (A related question here is whether these responses are associated with prior occasions when aggression was rewarded, or just manifestations of aggression in general.) *Desensitization* is said to occur after long-term exposure to violence on television: you see it so much it seems normal, so that seeing—or participating in—real violence is less offensive. Some say that films showing violence against women, sexual or otherwise, may lead to aggression against women by "normal" men (Donnerstein, 1984). But some research shows that viewing aggressive sexual acts actually results in less arousal than would be normal while watching non-aggressive sex, and that only rapists like scenes of rape (Abel, Barlow, Blanchard, and Gould, 1977).

There are important differences between the meanings and implications of the terms "prosocial behavior," "altruistic behavior," and "helping behavior." Any behavior that is valued by or helpful to the society in which the individual lives is *prosocial*. The key here, of course, is that an individual's "society" may not be society as a whole. What is good for a particular group (such as the "good samaritan" laws of Nazi Germany) may not be good for the rest of us. *Altruistic* behavior is "carried out to benefit another without anticipation of rewards from external sources" (Macaulay and Berkowitz, *Altruism and Helping Behavior,* 1970, p. 3). This basically means you would like to help because it will make other people better off, and has nothing to do with you personally. *Helping* behavior can be considered a subcategory of prosocial behavior, or even semi-altruistic, because this kind of action, while being of value to society or an individual, most likely does include obvious social rewards, that is to say, giving assistance to another with a definite goal in mind.

Three possible origins of helping behavior are identified by social scientists: sociobiological factors, cognitive developmental influences, and social learning. *Sociobiological* refers to an inborn instinct to help others. One group of sociobiologists refers to this as "kin selection"—helping members of the family because it will benefit future offspring; the further away from "kin" others are, the less helpful one is apt to be to them (Wilson, 1975). However, other sociobiologists disagree. They say that if "good" people continued to give their lives for the whole, then this genetic trait they carry would soon die out (Campbell, 1965).

According to the *cognitive developmental* viewpoint, the willingness to help others evolves in stages. The older one gets the less egocentric one becomes and the better able to take the other person's point of view. Underwood and Moore (1982) termed this "moral perspective-taking." Bar-Tal (1981) went a little further, saying that true altruistic behavior has to be totally voluntary and without thought of reward. At any rate, there does seem to be a strong connection between helping behavior and the level of cognitive development; for example, the older children get, the better able they are to socially interact.

Social learning refers to being taught to be helpful; it can come about either by someone else teaching you, or by learning from observing your environment—those around you. This view says that one learns to help in the same manner one learns all behaviors, through classical conditioning and operant conditioning, as well as social learning. An example of this could be that when a child does something which is thought by others to be a "good deed," he or she is praised for it—receives positive reinforcement—and this, of course, reinforces other positive responses.

I'm afraid the world is not a fair place. All anyone has to do is look around at the incomparable sorrow and pain that engulfs millions and millions of our fellow human beings to know, beyond all doubt, that the world is many things, but *fair* is not one of them. According to Lerner (1970, 1980, 1982), most people *do* believe that life is fair, that "most people get what they deserve" — an astonishing and quite harmful view.

Every once in a great while one is privileged to witness a truly altruistic act; it is awe-inspiring and humbling. But unfortunately, altruism is not a truly human characteristic. Like virtually all other living creatures, the human species is not evolving equally; some are farther along than others. Altruism is a "super-human" characteristic. The implications of the belief that "people get what they deserve" are unfortunate and continually apparent. When we see the beggar on the street, or the physically or mentally handicapped person, or the starving child with the bloated belly, most of us think that somehow, in some way, these people caused themselves to be the way they are; and because we are *not* like them, it makes us better, more deserving of the "good" life. Virtually everyone believes this way until it happens to them; then they cease believing that way. This attitude does not bode well for the "helping behavior."

Defining *loneliness* is not something that can be done succinctly. When we are not allowed to be with other people, we are lonely. When we are with other people but do not feel part of the group, we experience loneliness. When we are taken away from someone we care about, lonely feelings arise. A dictionary-like definition of loneliness would be: the unpleasant experience that occurs when a person's network of social relations is deficient in some important way, either quantitatively or qualitatively. There are basically two types of loneliness: social and emotional. Social loneliness occurs when one does not have a network of friends to interact with. Emotional loneliness is more intimate, having to do with the lack of a partner, or children, or parents to relate to. Loneliness can develop as the result of such things as a divorce or the death of a partner, physical separation from family and friends, and losing one's job. Some people simply seem predisposed to loneliness.

What kinds of contributions, if any, have social psychologists made to the understanding of *love*? Can love really be measured? I think any time a topic is studied contributions are made that will lead to a better understanding of that topic. Romantics say love is a mystery, and they would like to keep it that way. What is love? We have heard that "love rules the gods," "love is heaven," "love is a many-splendored thing," "love hurts," "fools fall in love," "love is complete agreement," "to know her is to love her," and so on and so on. All of these sentiments are probably partly true. Psychologists have defined liking as a *favorable attitude* toward another person, and love as a *deep attachment* to and caring for another person (Rukin 1974).

Studies by social psychologists have shown us that there are varying kinds of love—a fact we already knew, but that they solidified with research. For example, there is pseudo-passionate love and there is companionate love. Pseudo-passionate love is the type childish, immature people indulge in, the wild, uncontrollable melodramatic kind they show on television, the kind teenagers like to imitate. Companionate love is for adults, for people who are in for the long haul. There is certainly passion within it, but it is for the marathoner, not the short-distance person.

Philosophy

The philosophical concepts discussed in this section—formalism, hedonism, determinism, compatibilism, egoism, cultural relativism, and ethical relativism—relate to the processes governing thought and conduct. They seek to answer the questions of how we come to formulate what is right and what is wrong, how and why we make our laws governing civilization, why they are obeyed and why they are sometimes not obeyed. They address the concept of what makes a society workable and point to some possible causes of the breakdown of the social order. Foundationally, all of these propositions are inextricably connected with how consciousness perceives and reacts to its environment, that is to say, how it responds to the realization of its altered state of reality.

The thesis of *formalism* is basically that if it is right for one person to do something or to take a particular action, then it is right—all relevant conditions being the same—for another person to take the same action. It is an attempt to use the general concept of "universalization" to formulate true moral rules that apply universally. Although it is, of course, consistent, this is not a moral principle; it is a moral proposition which has consistency, as any valid proposition would. If it is right for a particular person to take a certain action under specific circumstances, then it is *always* right for a second or third or fourth person to take the same action, all else being the same. If someone says it is not a right action, then they must be able to defend why they think that is the case (Yandel, 1977).

The thesis of *hedonism* is that pleasure is the only thing intrinsically good and pain the only thing intrinsically evil. From this it follows that something has extrinsic value only to the extent that it increases pleasure or reduces pain; likewise, it has disvalue to the extent it increases pain or reduces pleasure. In the hedonist view, pleasures are simple conscious states which possess "positive hedonic tone"; pains are simple conscious states which possess "negative hedonic tone." Basically, an action is right if and only if it maximizes pleasure or reduces pain.

Some objections can be offered to hedonism. First of all, the theory itself cannot be considered complete. The question arises as to whose pain and whose pleasure we are talking about — that of the agent, of those affected by the action, or of those affected by the example the action sets? Also, two propositions entailed by hedonism need to be looked at closely: (1) It is necessary for an action to maximize pleasure in order to be right. (2) It is sufficient for an action to maximize pleasure in order to be right. Unless both those statements are true then the concept of hedonism is false (Eliot and Stern, 1979). However, that does not prevent a certain percentage of the population from adhering to such a belief.

Objections that can be offered to complex hedonism (intentional) center around implausibility. Actions can be shown to be right and not have anything to do with inducing pleasure. An action has value, it seems, independent of whether or not it has hedonic tone. It seems strained, at best, to indicate that the value lies in the reaction to an action and not in the action itself. In other words, the area of moral value in complex hedonism, as well as in simple hedonism (unintentional), seems to be focused in the wrong place — on the tones rather than on actions and persons. Indications are that it is false to imply that it is right to save a life simply because one or more persons may receive a positive hedonic tone from the performance of that action. These objections, and others relating to pleasure versus the capacity for pleasure, seem to be sound objections against hedonism.

If pleasure is good and pain is evil, that is still not enough to establish that hedonism is true. The hedonic tone (an altered state of reality), all alone, is said to be where the value lies. However, it would seem logical that *some* pleasures would rank higher than others. Then one gets into a matter of degrees, and hedonism seems to have a problem fitting this concept in with its description. It introduces a sort of "schizophrenia" into the topic. Some evasiveness seems to creep into the determination of "pleasure" and "pain."

Determinism holds that every basic human choice or action is an event. Therefore, any basic human choice or action is caused, and every basic human choice or action has a causal ancestor. To break this down a little: event A causes event B, which in turn causes event C. Therefore, the determinist must believe that if A does not occur, B cannot occur. In a further addition to the concept, A causes B if, and only if, the class of A-type events and the class of B-type events are in a one-to-one correlation. To reiterate, determinism holds that every event is caused, and so was its cause; therefore, every event has a causal ancestor. These processes (the chain of causation) do have some basic correlation to the events of construction and destruction (positive causes positive; negative causes negative).

Compatibilism holds, basically, that determinism is true, and that persons are responsible for their actions. The concept of "moral character" comes into play here; it involves making morally relevant choices and performing morally relevant actions. A person's moral character is determined by "character traits"—morally relevant traits and tendencies to believe in morally relevant ways. According to this view, one should be able to tell what kind of person someone is by knowing all of that person's character traits (Yandel, 1977).

Compatibilism is also called "soft determinism," indicating a close relationship between the two theories. The compatibilist believes that a person's responsibility for his or her moral character and resulting actions is enough to give "responsibility" all the sense it needs. The compatibilist also accounts for cases such as the kleptomaniac who "cannot help" stealing. Succinctly stated, the compatibilist holds that "S is responsible for doing A only if S can refrain from doing A; S can refrain from doing A if it is possible for one with S's IQ, physical abilities, and other qualities to do so." Another compatibilist response is to distinguish between the context and the content of the conscious states which cause actions for which we are responsible. For example: I want the car badly. I do not have the money to buy the car. It is wrong to take the car. Therefore, I cannot have the car.

Simply put, *egoism* is the doctrine that self-interest is the basis of all behavior. If an action enhances my self-interest it is a right action; it is wrong if, and only if, it negatively affects my self-interest. One can do much good for others and still be an egoist if that good done for others also benefits the egoist. This concept could relate to prosocial behavior, helpful behavior, or even altruistic behavior. Act morality considers what makes actions *right*. Agent morality considers what makes persons *praiseworthy*. Egoism is a theory of act morality: an action is right if and only if the agent who performed the action is morally praiseworthy for having done so. In this type of situation the results of the action might have a negative effect on one or more persons, but the action itself, in view of the information known, was the only right action available.

An egoist may certainly value the interest of another, if, for example: he or she likes the other person, so that self-interest is affected by the fate of the other person; the other person, whether liked or not, is so related to the egoist that one affects the other; helping the other will help the egoist; the egoist believes that the other's interests have *some* value but not as great as one's own. Another example: A man may be very nice or helpful to a very attractive woman. Whose interest does he really have in mind? Even if he does not actually expect any tangible reward (and I suspect most do not), his actions are motivated by self-interest. The limitations of egoism come into play because the egoist cannot accept the notion that any person has a self-interest that is as valuable as his or her own.

The thesis of *cultural relativism* is that not every society sees the same things as right or wrong. What is considered good or proper for one group of people may carry over to some other groups, but not to all. Similarly, what is considered wrong or bad in some societies is not seen that way in others (Keynes, 1986).

The thesis of cultural relativism is hard to appraise because of a number of problems. One main one is, how much leverage does one get or allow when defining an action? For example, what is killing? what is murder? what is the sex act? what is rape? Any or all of these actions may mean different things in different societies. How they are defined may determine if they are considered right or wrong. For validation of the cultural relativist thesis, one would need to come to the broad conclusion that since so many actions can be defined and judged in different ways, what is true of so many types of actions is probably true of *all* types of actions, and therefore, there is no type of action every society views as right and no type of action every society views as wrong.

The basic thesis of *ethical relativism* seems to be that one moral principle, idea, or concept is as valid as any other. It makes no difference which ones a society might follow; none are better and none are worse. Any possible choice between moral principles is simply an arbitrary endeavor.

Arguments in favor of ethical relativism relate to the idea that even if a moral principle were true or false, we could not tell which it was. The ambiguity in a numbers problem gives a good analogy. One number higher than any person has ever thought of is odd or is even. If one is true the other must be false; but we do not and cannot know which one is true and which is not. Similarly, this concept seems to imply that no moral principle is either true or false and that every moral principle is either true or false, but for no moral principle can we tell which it is. However, those statements are not logically compatible, and are therefore not good reasons for believing in ethical relativism. Since those reasons given seem to be the only possible good reasons for being an ethical relativist, then the logic is skewed at best, if not doubtful, ambiguous, obscure, and probably nonexistent. Nevertheless, one must remember that showing that there is no good reason for believing a particular claim does not prove the claim to be false (Yandel, 1977)!

The philosophical concepts that we have discussed in this section all have the power to influence or manipulate many of the actions of human individuals or groups. The initial actions decided upon cause further actions which result in a societal "rippling" effect and affect across the total spectrum of our "civilized" world.

Racism

> We are aware that it has become commonplace to pinpoint and describe the ills of our urban ghettos. The social, political and economic problems are so acute that even a casual observer cannot fail to see that something is wrong. While description is plentiful, however, there remains a blatant timidity about what to do to solve the problems [Carmichael and Hamilton, 1967, p. 164].

It is quite obvious that this statement by Stokely Carmichael about the condition of blacks in America is as relevant today as it was three decades ago. (The African-American population is referred to by different terms in different sectors of contemporary society. For the sake of consistency, I will use the term "blacks" throughout this section).

Most sources agree that the first blacks were brought to this country in large numbers by a Dutch man-of-war in 1661. From the time of the American Revolution until the invention of the cotton gin in 1793, considerable opposition to slavery and the slave trade developed in most of the states as far south as the Carolinas. This opposition came about in part from the embarrassing inconsistency between the struggle by white people for freedom from England and their holding black people as slaves (Logan, 1965). Also, the fact that black soldiers took part in the revolution in large numbers helped to strengthen the opposition to slavery.

The fact that blacks were slaves has an ongoing effect on everything that is their culture today. The first antislavery society was formed as far back as 1775 and the idea grew rapidly, especially in the North. However, the invention of the cotton gin reversed the trend toward the abolition of slavery in the southern states and virtually all attempts to end slavery in that region of the country had ceased to exist by the early nineteenth century.

At the same time the South was relying mainly on slavery to build an illusory prosperity, slavery was gradually disappearing in the North. By 1830 almost all northern states had outlawed slavery. This did not, however, mean that all was fine with blacks north of the Delaware-Maryland line. Even though there were more than a quarter of a million free blacks in the North by this time, racism and bigotry were just as prevalent there as anywhere else in America.

When the Civil War broke out in 1860, the cause was not simply slavery, although that was a part of it. Much of the reason had to do with the conflicts of interest between the industrial North and the agricultural South, as well as the doctrine of states' rights. Whatever the causes, victory by the North brought the emancipation of the slaves. President Lincoln's Emancipation Proclamation of 1862–63 proclaimed all the slaves free — except in those states or parts of states not in rebellion against the United States at that time. The Proclamation did not extend to all the states until after the North had won in 1865.

The Emancipation Proclamation was the first nationwide legal document put forth in an attempt to at least initiate the possibility of giving blacks equal rights under the law. After that came the Civil

Rights Act of 1866, the Fourteenth Amendment in 1868, the Civil Rights decision of 1883, the *Brown v. Board of Education* decision in 1954, the Voting Rights Act of 1965, and more than a dozen other amendments, court decisions, and laws relating to equal opportunities for black Americans (Logan, 1965).

Discrimination, against a great number of races, has a long history, but it seems that the black race has had the most difficulty of all. Why is this? Anthropologists agree that there is only one human species, known as *Homo sapiens;* but there are many varieties of the one species. These subspecies, or races, began evolving thousands of years ago through reproductive isolation brought about by geographical and cultural barriers. Today there is even some belief in the scientific community that *all* of us evolved from a single African woman (Associated Press, 1990). That possibility might be difficult to assimilate in some quarters. In 1987, Allan Wilson and Mark Stoneking of the University of California at Berkeley and Rebecca Cann of the University of Hawaii suggested all five billion people living today evolved from one single woman who lived in the sub-Saharan region of Africa about 200,000 years ago.

Whatever the origin of races, there is an undeniable history of blacks being set upon, to one degree or another, by white supremacists because of the whites' overestimation of the biological distinctions between the two human types (Pettigrew, 1975). Social distinctions often contribute to this overestimation. Differentials unfavorable to whites are explained away or ignored, while any differentials unfavorable to blacks—based on health, IQ, crime, and other statistics—are quickly interpreted as racially determined, without consideration of the vast disparities in opportunity between the groups. The unfortunate fact of the matter is that this particular way of thinking does seem to formulate itself, to a lesser or greater degree, in just about all of us. The human potential for racism is an established part of all human consciousness.

The operation of such conditions as poverty, impaired family life, and limited opportunities illustrate the fallacy involved. These social disabilities tend to result in more disease, lower scores on intelligence tests, and higher rates of crime regardless of race. Blacks as a group are poorer, come more often from broken homes, and are more likely to be victims of discrimination than any other Americans (Pettigrew, 1975).

At this date most of the "powers that be" indicate a sometimes begrudging recognition that it makes no sense to compare gross white and black data as a true test of anything, much less racial factors. It is hardly proper, for instance, to compare middle-class whites from intact homes with lower-class blacks from broken homes. Indeed, the economic floor for blacks is so distinctly below the floor of whites that nothing valid can come from comparing the two groups except to show the pitiful and shameful variance itself.

There are many issues one has to be aware of when trying to discover why making inroads into normal societal processes continues to be so extremely difficult for blacks; but three of the main areas concern stepfamilies and stepparenting, the cross-cultural perspective on normality, and, of course, the ethnic perspective. All of these areas have great impact on the black family because the negativity of those situations is so much more severe for blacks, as a group and individually, than for any other American racial group (Lemann, 1986).

Let us take a brief look at contemporary statistics. After some basic legislative, social, and economic gains were realized by the black population in America during the 1960s, a catastrophic plunge has taken place over the past twenty years, and most specifically during the past ten years. Poverty among black urban dwellers has risen 14 percent. The unemployment rate has nearly tripled in the past two decades (Lemann, 1986). The number of fatherless families has doubled among blacks during the last decade alone. The number of black families on welfare has increased by 200 percent. In today's inner cities, which are virtually all black, 75 percent of the people are poor, 65 percent are under 21 years of age, and only one in five families has a male head of the household.

There are several conflicting views as to why this "free fall" has taken place. One point of view is that blacks have been made worse off than before through dependency on more available welfare. Another answer is that blacks are too dependent on low-paying jobs for unskilled labor. When these began to dry up, with the closing of major industry, urban unemployment shot sky-high. A third view is that the flight of middle-class blacks from urban areas, beginning in the late sixties, left those that remained behind basically leaderless.

Recent studies indicate urban schools have become little more than armed camps (Associated Press, 1990). Street gangs have become the status of choice among inner-city youth, rather than academics or even sports. It seems that hope for the younger black generation has reached an all-time low, as seen in such things as an unparalleled increase in school dropout rates, drug use, and pregnancy among girls sixteen years old and under.

As stated earlier, part of the reason for the expansion of the ghetto phenomenon is thought to be that as the one-time leaders of those communities became more affluent and moved away, those who had to stay behind were left with nobody to direct them properly. Eldridge Cleaver wrote in his book *Soul on Ice* as long ago as 1969 that such a notion was a false, "white man's" idea. His argument is basically that the black population is the only one about which a statement like that could be made and given any credence. Therefore, that implication alone seems to indicate very clearly that it is not a concept which will stand too much scrutiny.

The American black experience is unlike almost any other in human history. Blacks cannot directly and comfortably relate to the basic concept of being a "native son" (Carmichael and Hamilton, 1967). We might say that is not true, that they *are* natives of this land and *can* feel that they are. The fact of the matter is, however, that they cannot. This situation affects blacks' feelings of patriotism. Those who want and need the camaraderie of "rallying round the flag" have a hard time being let in, at least all the way, and the rest do not want in at all.

The answers to all of these problems are still being sought. I do believe, however, that the mass media, both print and electronic, contribute to a large number of *wrong* answers. If we as a nation could get a more controlling hand on this aspect of modern society, we may go a long way toward alleviating the problem. The benefits of the mass media could be enormous (Toffler, 1980). But how does one go about utilizing them properly without getting into censorship? It would seem to me that education is the most workable tool we have available to us.

The "news," in all its forms, is what most people take to be the facts. In actuality, the news is no less entertainment than virtually anything else in the media. The success of a news program or a newspaper depends on how many people watch or read it. Every time a newsperson gets the idea for a story, the first question is how to grab the audience. High drama is an important — maybe the most important — part of the story. The result is that every single major news story that comes out every single day is filled with outright errors and misleading information.

Utilizing the media in conjunction with education can insure that helpful and corrective information can get out to the largest number of people in the shortest period of time. The world is in the midst of an information explosion never even dreamed of until recently. More people know more about more things than at any other time in the history of the world. If at least some of this knowledge could be used to address the problems discussed in this section, it is quite possible that real progress would be made.

Proper dissemination and assimilation of educational information on the negative influences on the black population—drugs, the "babies having babies" syndrome, students dropping out of school, the perpetuation of low self-esteem, etc.—would definitely have a positive influence on changing the status quo. The teaching of marketable skills for better job placement and the reeducation of those in positions of power (possibly the most difficult task of all) could have a very successful ripple effect on the situation as a whole. We will delve further into the topic of media negligence in Chapter 8.

In recent years there have been any number of propositions put forth by learned individuals in an attempt to contribute to solving this major problem in American life. There is the idea that if the everyday person on the street were able to obtain more political power the situation would change for the better (Savitch, 1975). This point of view observes that blacks have comparatively little political influence and suggests that if they could somehow band together as a single unit they would be a force to be reckoned with. There is an obvious validity to that idea.

Another partial solution proposed is that of providing, as a beginning, adequate housing for all blacks, so that they would at least have a stable place to call home while going about trying to rectify some of the other problems (Forman, 1978). This idea was put forth many years ago and is still mostly in the "planning" stage as we approach the twenty-first century. One possible way of doing this involves not tearing down old houses while building new ones, resulting in *more* houses. If that could be accomplished, the merits of proposed solutions such as urban homesteading, rent subsidies, federal loans at low interest rates, and additional public housing could be more productively explored. The basic idea is that we can help blacks more than we are now helping them, if we really try, if that is what we really want to do.

There is also the view that simply removing discriminatory barriers to employment will not benefit the many blacks who are unprepared for anything but low-skilled jobs in the first place. There is also a lot of discussion about the inadequacies of the welfare system; some believe that welfare dependency simply feeds on itself, becoming an attempt at perpetual survival. It should also be said that a growing number of blacks themselves are strongly advancing the point of view that the role of "victim" in black society is, in many instances, a coveted one (Loury, 1990). Not having to take responsibility for failure at the personal level means not being able to take responsibility for success at the personal level.

There are those that say blacks who make excuses for their "shortcomings," or for others of the black race, are themselves guilty of racism (Thomas, 1990). An example is the reaction to the arrest of the mayor of Washington, D.C., Marion Barry, for smoking crack cocaine. NAACP leader Benjamin Hooks believed the charges against Barry might have been part of a conspiracy to drive black politicians out of important government offices. Reporter Courtland Milloy, who is black, wrote a column in the *Washington Post* titled "Bearing the Burden of Being the Black Mayor of the White Man's Plantation."

As reported by Cal Thomas in the *San Antonio Light* of January 30, 1990, Milloy tried to blame Barry's behavior on his roots, saying that he had been physically and verbally abused by white racists. Thomas went on to say that black leadership should stop apologizing for blacks who are crooks. He said that ethics, honor, duty, and integrity are standards that apply to all men and women and that to excuse blacks under the guise of racism is simply another form of racism. This mind-set, he concluded, is at least in part responsible for the slow progress of integration.

The overwhelming evidence today, however, indicates that the shadow of unequal treatment of the black population, both overt and covert, continues to hold sway over much of this country's economic, political, and social life. Consider these facts: In a single city in a single year—Dallas, Texas, in 1989—the convictions of six persons sentenced to long prison terms were overturned on the grounds of wrongful arrest and indictment; all of those people were black (Associated Press, 1990). Recently, the Selma, Alabama, public schools were closed after several hundred black students walked out to protest the firing of the black superintendent of schools. In Los Angeles,

79 percent of all persons who died violently in 1989 were black. In the ghetto area of New York City a black man between the ages of 16 and 35 is more likely to suffer a drug-related death than to die from any other cause (UPI, 1990). The list could go on and on. The negative bias against blacks in virtually every meaningful area is simply irrefutable, and growing daily. The black population in America totals about 30 million people, about 12 percent of the total. Simple mathematics indicate that, in this country at least, the black race is not the "norm." Consequently, it would be impossible for blacks' family situations, taken as a whole, to be "normal," that is to say, average. Therefore, the underlying structure of the American black experience, in relation both to itself and to the outside world, must be dealt with in the context of those differences (McGoldrick, Pearce, and Giordano, 1982).

Martin Luther King III has indicated (Omni, 1990) that the fullest extent of civil and human rights may only come to the black population when it is able to coalesce into a double power base, one in the area of massive voter registration, the other in the arena of consumerism. If 30 million people can come together as virtually one giant buyer in this capitalist society, the potential positive influence for that group could be staggering.

A recently concluded 30-year study has, it seems to me, an interesting correlation to the multifaceted structure of what we call "normal family processes." The research involved the tracking of nearly 700 nonwhite children who grew up in poverty, without specific parental direction, with no means of educational support, and on the receiving end of much bigotry (Scientific American, 1989). The study found that the great majority of these children have grown up to be normal, productive members of society. One main thread ran throughout this success story. The more structured and stable and caring the home environment was, regardless of whether or not the caregivers were parents, the more competence the children displayed, the more confidence they acquired, and the more successful they were in assimilating into "normal" adult life. The great majority of information gathered on this most difficult of social problems seems to indicate that an important part of the solution — the change of a negative reality to a positive reality — depends on the individual family system and home structure.

Along with the many tangible causes of the obstacles to black assimilation into the American mainstream, there is another, less clearly indicated, but maybe even more insidious: In America there is a perpetual myth that because one is better off financially, somehow he or she is a better person. A clinging human concept whispers to us that we are "lucky" or "unlucky," better or worse off, in direct relation to whether we are somehow "good" or "bad" people. The result of this most heinous of ideas is the belief that *we* have good lives because we deserve it, and *they* have horrible lives because they deserve it.

Nearly 150 years ago, the philosopher John Stuart Mill stated a truth that still applies today:

> Of all vulgar modes of escaping from the consideration of the effect of social and moral influences on the human mind, the most vulgar is that of attributing the diversities of conduct and character to inherent natural differences [Mill, (1848) 1899, p. 390].

Comparatively speaking, we have just recently pulled ourselves out of the primordial ooze . . . and it shows.

Work

To work is to put forth effort. It is to labor, toil, and strive. It is what humans do in order to make their way in life. (Other animals are sometimes said to "work" also. However, a purpose of this chapter is to remain within the arena and consciousness of *Homo sapiens.*) A vocation is a particular profession, business, or occupation, that is to say, the individual vocation is the specificity of the work. But why does work take place? The obvious answers could be, to make a living, to feed one's family, to be able to buy things—at its most basic, to be able to continue to exist. If you don't work you don't eat; if you don't eat you die. But indications are that the situation is much more complex.

In today's society, much of the time, the work environment consists of more than one person. It did in past societies also, but does so even more today. A workplace often consists of a group of people. Groups have been studied by social psychologists for more than 50 years (Penrod, 1986). It would seem to be an obvious statement to say that groups (that is, the people in groups) mutually influence each other. However, the possibilities are more diverse than that. Floyd Allport (1924), in his classic social psychology textbook, said that "nobody ever stumbled over a group," implying that groups are illusory, existing only in people's minds. However, there are other studies which indicate groups have quite tangible boundaries. Take the following scenario: Several people are talking together in the middle of a school hallway. You have to pass them on the way to your classroom. Would you take the straightest route, which leads you directly into their midst, or would you walk around them? Further, would you consider these interacting people blocking the hall as so many individuals, each constituting a separate obstacle to be negotiated on your way to class, or would you treat this collection of people as something more, having a certain life of its own, which you recognize by walking around the entire collection—the *group*?

In a study conducted by Eric S. Knowles (1973) which set up a hallway situation like the one above, it was found that more people walked around the group than through it. Of further interest were findings that more people walked through two-person groups than through four-person groups, and more people walked through groups of people of lower status (in this case, college students) than through groups of people of higher status (college professors). These findings indicate, basically, not only that groups have tangible boundaries but that group boundaries vary in permeability depending on the size and status of the group. Groups also have the ability to perceive as a single unit and react as a single unit; examples would be gangs, the military, and minorities.

In the work environment one can find employees divided into groups. In many cases these are "task" groups. Personnel professionals in industry and business are certainly aware of the positive effects on productivity of group identification—for example, a number of people assigned to perform one or more tasks together. There has been much research into group camaraderie as an important part of success in workplace accomplishments (Steiner, 1972). This seems to have a lot to do with a shared task resulting in a shared reward. In addition, groups also feel "shared" harm.

Is work satisfaction closely related to life satisfaction? Is that one of the main reasons people work? Although income, in and of itself, does not appear to be the dominant factor in life satisfaction, it is clear that gainful employment and the economic security it provides do affect the quality of life (Flanagan, 1987). A lack of income, by any measure, is a major part of life dissatisfaction. Indications are that life satisfaction is, in fact, part of the overall reason behind why we work. (It probably is not necessary to state that practically every situation in life must be stated in the virtual sense.)

It probably can be said with some credibility that the majority of people who work do so to fulfill one or more of the following needs: economic needs, belonging needs, the need to feel a sense of self-worth, the need to serve others, the need for self-development or self-expression, the need to comply with a multiplicity of social standards, or simply the overall need to be needed. It might be said that another reason why we work is out of a kind of guilt. People who work are good. People who don't work are bad: "bums," "welfare queens," the homeless. "He was a hard-working man" is universally meant as a positive statement. "The guy can't hold a job" is always meant as a negative comment. A very important part of our value system is related to our positive attitude toward work, known as the "work ethic." It has been said that while work is necessary it actually has no intrinsic value (Michelozzi, 1988). Work has value only within the context of the amount of value individuals attach to it. (The same, of course, could be said of just about everything.) Work is a learned thing. Some people learn it (are programmed for it) better than others.

The following passage from the textbook *Coming Alive from Nine to Five* (Michelozzi, 1988) is a good example of another view:

> Edward Kennedy recounts how, during his first campaign for the U.S. Senate, his opponent said scornfully in a debate, "This man has never worked a day in his life!" Kennedy says that the next morning as he was shaking hands at a factory gate, one worker leaned toward him and confided, "You ain't missed a goddamned thing" [p. 32].

Recent indications are that something has gone wrong at the workplace (Pascarella, 1984). It seems that the cause of much of the frustration on the job is not related to too much work or being worked too hard. The major complaint by workers is that they are not allowed to contribute in any significant way. No one listens to their ideas about how things might be done better. They are not given enough respect (U.S. Chamber of Commerce, 1985). A little more than a hundred years ago a man was considered very lucky if his work provided a living for the family and was also satisfying.

Today satisfaction has become an integral part of the vocational picture.

It may very well be that work and its integration within the human condition are nothing more than a "selection by consequences" resulting from behavioral reinforcement (Skinner, 1987). Even if that is the actual truth of the situation, it does not change the *fact* of the situation. We humans *have* worked, do *now* work, and will *continue* to work, in one form or another, for the foreseeable future. That fact, coupled with multiple indications that the definition and description of what work is and who does it is today changing drastically, indicates the need for much preparation for the future.

The general structure of the "traditional" American family, in which the husband-father is the provider and the wife-mother the homemaker, began to take shape early in the nineteenth century. This structure lasted about 150 years, from the 1830s to 1980, when the U.S. Census Bureau no longer automatically denominated the male as head of the household (Bernard, 1985). This, of course, was the result of more and more women entering the work force, especially married women. The problems and challenges in that area are ongoing.

There have been costs and rewards for both men and women within the contemporary work situation. The pluses seem to have a lot to do with the "equal" sharing of family rights and responsibilities (although there is still much debate on that issue). For men, the most serious cost has perhaps been a loss of identification with maleness, not only at the work site but at home as well. "The American male looks to his breadwinning role to confirm his manliness" (Brenton, 1966, p. 12). When the man's total responsibility for this breadwinning role was taken away some major adjustments were in order. A major theme relating to the constraints work places on families revolves around time and timing, that is to say, the scheduling of work and the timing of demands. Many demands of work now go well beyond the 40-hour week and even draw other family members in as vital players in the occupational world (Kanter, 1985). The result is a limited amount of time left for personal or familial pursuits, which becomes a considerable source of strain on the family system. In order to keep the family from becoming dysfunctional, many new types of arrangements within the working structure of the system are now coming to the fore.

Employed women who become pregnant are now receiving much attention in both the family and work arenas. A recent study shows some concern pertaining to perceptions of how much husbands *think* they help in this situation and how much wives believe their husbands have actually been helpful (Gray, Lovejoy, Piotrkowski, and Bond, 1990). The authors looked at 490 married mothers of infants working full-time, to determine the relationship of husbands' supportiveness to the wives' well-being; comparisons were made before and after pregnancy. Most women reported that they thought their husbands were supportive but not as much so as they could have been. The husbands, on the other hand, thought they were very supportive—a definite case of different realities.

Another challenge for the married female worker relates to child care. A survey of parents of school-age children in Boston revealed that most parents were unable to be home every day when their children returned from school (Seligson, Marshall, and Marx, 1990). Many children spend at least part of the day being cared for by siblings.

Indications are that inflexible workplace policies and schedules often create child-care difficulties for parents. A large number of households, most particularly low-income families, are paying as much as 15 percent of their total income for school-age child care. The results point to the possibility that business and government might have to become more involved in providing these services. In these cases, "collective" consciousness changes must take place. However, differing perceptions of reality keep people at odds on these issues.

There are, of course, numerous other issues having to do with the contemporary workplace. The basic structure of the entity and the methodology of the process are changing literally on a daily basis. Not only are there major convulsions within current vocational circles, but what the future holds is also of high interest. The answers to such questions as who will and will not be working in the twenty-first century, as well as what work will consist of, are being formulated at this very moment.

Many things are changing, but some things are not. Child labor, for example, and all the negativity that it brings, reached its peak in this country during the 1890s (Center, 1990). But today, nationwide, U.S. labor officials say more than 22,000 children are working illegally (United States Labor Department, 1990). That figure is the highest since the Fair Labor Standards Act was passed in 1938. Many of these children are identified as recent immigrants; a smaller percentage are blacks and other native-born minorities. Interestingly, this mixture is quite similar to that of working children during the last century.

The noted behaviorist and controversial psychologist B. F. Skinner states (1987) that most people in the Western democracies enjoy a reasonable degree of affluence, freedom, and security. However, it seems that, more than ever before, they are bored, listless, or depressed. They do not like their lives. They—that is, *we*—do not like their (our) work. Skinner identifies this as a possible result of being "alienated from the product of their labor" (p. 177). That is to say, they get no positive reinforcement from the results of their work because they do not even know what those results are.

It would seem to me that from the time our ancestors decided to discontinue being quadrupedal, lying within the bosom of the recently evolved *Homo sapiens* was the desire to do whatever it took to stay alive—that is, work. Much of the time work was mandatory; some of the time it was fun. It remains similar to this very day. Now, however, a person's need for a vocation to also be something he or she enjoys doing—gets personal positive reinforcement from—is stronger than it has ever been during our past history. In fact, the need may be so strong and so important as to be simply necessary for continued survival, at least as we know it.

Alvin Toffler, in his book *The Third Wave* (1980), took a provocative glimpse into the future, noting such potential changes as the superseding of industrial mass production, the rise of the home-centered society, the redefining of the corporation, and the end of nine-to-five work schedules. Just 15 years later many of these predictions are already beginning to come into being. What the next ten years will bring should be quite exciting.

The great majority of information, both empirical and otherwise, indicates that more leisure time does not mean more happiness. However, what one does that makes one feel worthwhile does translate into a more positive life. The trick, it seems, is to make what one gets paid money to do, and what one believes is a worthwhile endeavor, the same thing. The old adage says that "any work is better than no work." Within the realm of human consciousness, that may, in fact, be a harmful myth.

The author Studs Terkel put it eloquently:

Work is a search for daily meaning as well as daily bread, for recognition as well as cash, for astonishment rather than torpor; in short, for a sort of life rather than a Monday through Friday sort of dying. Perhaps immortality, too, is part of the quest [Terkel, 1972, p. xiii].

CHAPTER 7

Positive Altered States

Existential-Realism

As mentioned to some extent earlier, positivity as well as negativity has been born out of "altered states" of reality derived from overall consciousness. A major example is the human need and striving to understand what it really means to be human. This causes us to search for our "identity." We try to find the true definition, on a personal level, of such terms as responsibility, choices, anxiety, awareness, and death. This search and striving, derived from a particular state of consciousness, has been labeled "existentialism," which is both a philosophy and a form of therapy.

Closely connected to existentialism, with a similar relationship to the field of counseling, is a practice known as reality therapy. Its basic philosophy is also predicated on the assumption that people are ultimately self-determining and in charge of their own lives. A major part of reality therapy's focus is based on the principles of social learning theory (see Chapter 1). This explains that behavior is learned mostly through imitation and reinforcement. In relation to consciousness it is important to note that our *perception* determines our concept of "reality," and therefore determines our concept of the object of imitation and of the reinforcer. Bringing these two positive forces together may form a "whole" that is considerably stronger and more worthwhile than the two separate parts. I call this alliance "existential-realism."

Existentialism

Existentialism in literature and its development as a philosophy began to take shape in the early to mid–nineteenth century in Europe.

There were, of course, some earlier existential works, but this time period will suffice as a general starting point (Karl and Hamalian, 1963). The movement is said to have begun as a response to the modernization of humankind and civilization, which resulted in less control of self and more dependency on the external world. The central emphasis in literary works was on the alienation of people from an absurd world, their recognition of the world as meaningless, and their need to distinguish between the authentic and the unauthentic self. This is what Rollo May (1983) refers to when he says late twentieth century humankind is dying from "inauthenticity" because our greatest fear is ostracism, that is, we allow the external world to determine our personal worth. May goes on to say that this feeling of inauthenticity is possibly most clearly expressed in the fear of castration, that is, the fear of "losing" one's self.

Existentialism is a "mind-set" that can be said to be, at least in large part, a philosophy of disorientation. This would correlate most succinctly to existentialist writing as a literature of despair. Some examples of existentialist writings are *The Grand Inquisitor*, by Feodor Dostoyevsky; *Memoirs of a Lunatic*, by Leo Tolstoy; *The Bucket Rider*, by Franz Kafka; *Socrates Wounded*, by Bertolt Brecht; and *The Stranger*, by Albert Camus. All these works paint a remorseful picture of lost souls held prisoner in a meaningless and ridiculous world.

A closer look at existentialism reveals that meaninglessness and despair are only one part of its total world view. In fact, larger tenets of the philosophy state that these conditions need to be and can be overcome. Jean-Paul Sartre (1957) states that existentialism has been wrongly accused of inviting people to remain in a kind of desperate quietism, feeling that any action is quite useless and therefore should not even be attempted. Sartre goes on to say that "most people who use the word would be rather embarrassed had they to explain it" (p. 11). His point is that when we as a species begin to understand that salvation and meaning come only from within ourselves, then we will also conjointly begin to understand how to formulate a way out of the morass of uselessness. The key is that we as individuals are the only ones who have the power to accomplish such a task.

The founding tenets of existentialism as it relates to the human condition are (1) freedom and responsibility, (2) anxiety as a condition of living, (3) self-awareness, (4) death and nonbeing, (5) the search for meaning, (6) self identity and meaningful relationships (Corey, 1991; May, 1983; Yalom, 1989). "Self-awareness" is also a definition of consciousness. To understand consciousness is to understand what it means to be human. And to understand what it means to be human is also the primary search of existentialism.

In existentialism, the terms "freedom and responsibility" relate to the fact that we as humans are free to make choices about how we will conduct our lives. This allows us control over the kind of lives we live. Therefore, since we do have these choices, we must also take responsibility for them. Consequently, wherever and however we end up, we had a choice in being there. That said, existentialism does take into account inner and outer possibilities—for example, biological and environmental determinants—that are not within the realm of human control.

Anxiety basically comes from our awareness of the human condition as finite. This, of course, is a positive thing because it forces us to take action in some manner. Death and nonbeing are connected with awareness as well as anxiety. Being aware that one will die gives value to living. A singularly human capability is the ability to understand the concept of the future and the inevitability of death. To know how to conduct life, one must know about death.

A critical evaluation of the concepts of existential philosophy and existential psychotherapy lends itself well to several possibilities. We know *about* death, but we do not *know* death. Critics of existentialism take issue with the idea of death denial. They say, "We don't deny death. Everyone knows they are going to die." In his book *Love's Executioner* (1989), Irvin Yalom shows that is not actually true. All people who are alive think only *other people* die. We know on a conscious level, but on a subconscious level we do not know. Yalom says that during his many years of work with cancer patients facing imminent death, he found the patents used two very common and very powerful self-deceptions to alleviate the fear of death. One is the belief that the individual is special; the other is the belief in an ultimate rescuer. A person can live more fully only when these delusions are put to rest.

Existential Psychotherapy

Psychotherapy is primarily a human encounter (Van Kaam, 1966). If that encounter is to be authentic the therapist, at least for their time together, must be totally present with the client. What better way to understand the client's world view than to "take part in" that existence? Consequently, from a purely logical as well as philosophical point of view, the guidelines for existentialist therapy stand up to close scrutiny and criticism more than adequately.

The actions of all humans, in one way or another, reflect their philosophical bases (Arbuckle, 1975). Therefore, if one's basic beliefs are governed, for instance, by the concept of individual freedom and individual responsibility, or by phenomenology or humanism, or by existentialist views on anxiety and nonbeing, then one's words and actions will mirror that viewpoint. As a result, a therapeutic endeavor that utilized this understanding should culminate in a positive life-restructuring outcome.

Existentialist tenets have something to offer virtually all clinicians, regardless of their theoretical orientation (Yalom, 1989). Existential therapy offers a way of explaining a multitude of varying clinical data and to formulate any number of more specific strategies pertaining to "psychowellness." Yalom agrees with a number of other practitioners and researchers when he states that one of the most important contributions of existential therapy is the value it puts on the human quality of the one-on-one therapeutic relationship (Yalom, 1989).

One of the main criticisms levelled at the existentialist approach is that it is too ethereal or intellectual. B. F. Skinner (1980) even called it more analogous to poetry than to science. I will risk being presumptuous by stating that Dr. Skinner's allusion must have been made with tongue firmly planted in cheek. The theory's precepts are quite basic and logical. However, the argument could be made that the less abstract thinking ability the client might have, the more difficult this human-centered therapy might be for him or her. At the same time, I believe a good argument could also be made against that notion, especially when combining existentialism with the precepts of reality therapy.

Existentialism began to develop into a method of psychotherapy and social intervention in Europe during the 1930s (Corey, 1991). This came about basically as a reaction to both psychoanalysis and behaviorism, the first being overly steeped in unconscious forces, the second aligning itself too closely with sociocultural conditioning. Three of the initiators of existential psychotherapy in Europe were Medard Boss, Viktor Frankl, and Ludwig Binswanger. The two persons believed to have been most significant in bringing the existential approach to the United States are Rollo May and Irvin Yalom. Concerning therapeutic technique pertaining to existentialism, May laid out some very specific groundwork in his book *The Discovery of Being* (1983). As an indication of how he personally felt about *too much* technique, May coined the hybrid word "methodolatry."

A large number of existential therapists are not terribly concerned with technique. In contrast to many current modes of operation, understanding comes first, then more specific application. May says that without understanding, technical methodology is not even relevant. After understanding, what is technically important relates to the following questions: What will work best in revealing the existence of the client at this exact moment? How can one best put a spotlight on the client's current being in the world? These issues are surrounded by the question of how to evolve a clear understanding of working within this in-the-moment context.

Yalom (1980) suggests there are four main givens relevant to existential psychotherapy: the inevitability of death, the freedom to make our lives as we will, our ultimate aloneness, and the complete absence of any meaning to life. Out of psychotherapy comes the wisdom of what these things actually mean. Out of wisdom comes redemption. Out of redemption comes a positive, useful, "altered" state of consciousness.

In practical application, the overall philosophy of existentialism could work as an encompassing umbrella. Underneath that umbrella, an integration with more specificity would fit well. This is where reality therapy and some additional guidelines, which we will also bring together in this chapter, come into play. The main idea is that once one comes to understand what "being truly human" actually means, then the pathway to a healthy, constructive, and productive life opens up to a more clearly assessable view.

During any application of existentialist therapy, the thing to keep in mind, it seems to me, is what existentialism stands for. Regardless of the presenting problem, the "client" (whether that be one person or a whole country) is slowly taken through the concepts of awareness, freedom, responsibility, identity, relationship to others, the search for meaning, anxiety, and death and nonbeing. This is done as each one relates to the dysfunction of contemporary living. Explanations are given to those who have been mentally wounded in the "authentic" manner previously described. The core of the existentialist approach is to take existence seriously (May, 1981). As living, breathing humans we really know only two things: one, we will all be dead someday, and two, we are not dead now. The all-important question is, what shall we do between those two points? The appropriate target populations for potential intervention could be quite varied. The following thought from Sartre (1957) may give an idea as to who might benefit from existential therapy:

> Not only is man what he conceives himself to be, but he is also what he wills himself to be after this thrust toward existence. Man is nothing else but what he makes of himself. Such is the first principle of existentialism [p. 14].

Let me solidify the target-population question even further with a quotation from Rollo May (1981):

> No matter how great the forces victimizing the human being, man has the capacity to know that he is being victimized, and thus to influence in some way how he will relate to his fate. There is never lost that kernel of the power to take some stand, to make some decision, no matter how minute [p. 22].

Both of the preceding quotations very directly allude to the notion that humankind is in basic control of its destiny. People have been the formulators of "what is." We can also be the formulators of "what can be." That proposition takes in virtually the entire spectrum of those who may have a need to "redesign" their lives.

As an addendum to our discussion of the practical application of existential therapy, it must be said that there are detractors who doubt its effectiveness in multicultural counseling. I believe that opinion to be erroneous also. It would be quite simplistic for a therapist and client to attempt to build or restructure a more positive emotional life in isolation from tradition, history, and culture. These factors belong to the very "existence" of the counselee (Van Kaam, 1966). The client always remains to some degree an important part of his or her tradition, and is undeniably dependent on it. Thus, the multiplicities of tradition are the embodiment of "coexistentialism" (the combining of culture to therapy). Indeed, "the existentialist approach is particularly suited to the understanding of, for example, the Chicano personality as it follows the psychology of indigenous peoples of Mexico" (Medina, 1974). Existentialism is a pathway, in its very essence, which all humans can follow to become more fully human.

Pain and longing are the primal ingredients of which we humans are made (Frankl, 1967). We are continually searching for something, anything, that will tell us that our being here matters in some small way. An understanding of "being-consciousness" can come about through the adventure open to us through existential psychotherapy. It can be a treacherous journey, horrifyingly frightening. However, when one becomes successful at peeling away what we know to be the "normal" human context of living, the result can be an illuminating salvation of the soul.

Reality Therapy

The basic theoretical foundation of reality therapy is also firmly attached to the premises of choices and responsibility. This type of approach is sometimes referred to as the psychological version of the "three R's"—responsibility, right-and-wrong, and reality. The one person who is thought of as the founder of reality therapy is William Glasser (see Glasser, 1965).

Responsibility is basically the ability to give to or obtain for yourself those things that you wish to have in order to fulfill your needs as an individual—with the proviso that you should not infringe upon others' ability to fulfill their own needs and wishes. A person acts responsibly because of a need to have other persons feel good about him or her. It is also important to proceed in a fashion that will allow good feelings by him or herself. To quote Glasser, "people do not act irresponsibly because they are ill, they are 'ill' because they act irresponsibly" (Glassett, 1975, p. 19).

Despite the varying ways that psychological problems tend to manifest themselves, Glasser believes they are all the result of one main factor: an inability to fulfill one's basic needs. There is a connection between a person's lack of success in meeting these needs and the amount of distress he or she is faced with in life. Glasser states that all psychological problems can be related to the fact that people deny the reality of the world environment around them.

The areas of *right and wrong* fit into this ongoing pitfall quite well. In human terms, what constitutes right and wrong is always difficult to pin down. For the most part, it simply means that we must maintain a decent, satisfactory standard of behavior. If we do not live our lives within the boundaries of what are considered moral and ethical limitations, then the esteem of others, which is an innate part of a healthy growth pattern, will be withheld and self-worth will suffer. The final member of the "three R's," *reality*, is possibly the most difficult to be completely specific about. In the simplest of terms it seems to be mostly a matter of denial. Whatever an individual's emotional problem, whatever the unacceptable behavior or how it manifests itself, the person in question is denying the reality of the surrounding world. This constitutes a "negative altered state." Some are lawbreakers, which is a denial of the rules of society. Some are rude, or bullies, or troublemakers, which is denying the rules of social interaction. And some believe they are being plotted against by virtually everyone, which is a denial of the rules of common sense.

In the past decade or so many people have come to believe that the earlier forms of psychotherapeutic methodology have brought on a generation of irresponsible and parent-hating children. Those types of therapy almost always said that it was the fault of someone else—parents, teachers, bad friends, surroundings, or other influences (Sundberg, 1973). The result of this, of course, could never be to make better and stronger children. It would, and will, always result in weaker and less accountable human beings.

In reality therapy, the present and the future are given the most attention and the past is largely ignored. No real importance is tied to the unconscious; however, consciousness, in its most literal sense, is quite integral. Transference is not used as a therapeutic tool. Reality therapy places great emphasis on the moral issues of right and wrong. Finally, possibly the most important issue of all in reality therapy is that it is looked on as a *teaching* process, not a healing process (Thompson and Rudolph, 1988).

To conclude this outline of the theory, reality therapy relates most specifically to the concepts of human needs—such as the need to feel worthy, the need to be in control of one's life, the need for love, and the need for joy—and responsibility, which emphasizes positive actions in achieving these fundamental needs.

In critical evaluations of the concept of reality therapy, the majority of complaints relate to some of the theory's central tenets, as stated above. That is to say, some consider the approach to be

lacking because it does not emphasize the power of the past, the unconscious, transference, the effect of negative experiences in early
childhood, and even possibly the therapeutic value of dreams (Corey,
1991). The problems many find with reality therapy seem to relate
to its almost total focus on *consciousness*. That, of course, is the
whole idea, and a major precept of this book. However, many critics
feel that this method does not deal properly with the conflicts of
repression and the influence of the unconscious on how we behave,
choose, think, and feel. That is true, and purposely so. The main
theme of existentialism and reality therapy—and thus of existential-
realism—is that, basically, we behave, think, and feel how we
"choose" to behave, think, and feel.

The practical application and therapeutic techniques of reality
therapy are manifested in accordance with the major precepts.
Under the umbrella of those procedures that lead to change would
lie the mandate to explore wants, needs, and perceptions. Along
with that, the counselor would need to get the client to evaluate
his or her own behavior as objectively as possible and make sure
that most of the focus was on current happenings. The counselor's
personal involvement with the client, as well as planning and com-
mitment, would be quite integral to the success of these procedures.

To be more specific, the exploration of wants, needs, and perceptions, for example, would depend on the counselor's skill at questioning the client so as to obtain a good idea of what the client's
needs are and how to meet them. This means being noncritical and
accepting of the client's perception of problems and solutions. Also
important in this connection is creating a supportive environment.
One of the most workable ways to do this is to begin to understand
and relate to the client through his or her world view, that is, *consciousness* (Glasser, 1969, 1975; Corey, 1991).

In relating to the even more specific lineage of a particular set
of steps to follow, existential-realism therapy would continue very
much along these lines:

1. Build a good relationship with the client.
2. Investigate all present behavior in an accepting manner.
3. Help the client to evaluate what is going on in his or her life
   and what it is he or she needs.
4. Look for other ways to get for the client what he or she wants.

5. Help the client begin choosing alternatives and making commitments.
6. Evaluate and investigate the validity of those commitments.
7. Go over in good detail the logical consequences of not achieving and also of holding commitments and achievement as they relate to reaching goals.

The basic foundation is to understand what are responsible and irresponsible actions. The client must come to conclusions about what has positive and negative personal impact. He or she must understand the concept of choices and alternatives, must become aware of the relationship between needs and commitments, and must make behavior changes in order to allow for positive adjustment to the real world. As this is done, an initiation of the third part of the therapeutic puzzle—right and wrong determination—will automatically come into being. This total process then enables the client to move in the direction of finally getting what he or she wants. It is also important to remember all the while the therapist's role as teacher and model.

The target population to whom existential-realism therapy might be applicable is wide and varied. There is much precedent indicating the positive use of reality therapy in such areas as improving the classroom behavior of disruptive children; helping students who are experiencing learning and behavioral problems; working with adult offenders, emotionally disturbed patients, and institutionalized adolescents; improving teaching methods at the elementary, junior high, and high school level in public as well as private schools; and helping learning disabled children (Cohen and Itzhak, 1984; Thompson and Rudolph, 1988).

The goals of group counseling would fit quite well into reality therapy's tenets also. The members as a whole and as individuals have a specific focus. What they want to get out of the process is usually relatively clear. The groups are generally problem-oriented. Often the challenge is to initiate growth and tap unknown potential. The advantages resulting from such concepts are reached, in great part, through support, understanding, feedback, direction, and empathy.

In its use and understanding of such terms as choices, responsibility, alternatives, needs, and "the here and now," reality therapy is, again, much in line with existential philosophy. We may not be able to control the "real" world, but we can control how we perceive it and react to it.

In his more recent works Glasser has introduced an umbrella prescription he calls "control theory." It simply provides a conceptual framework for reality therapy. The overall premise is that although outside events influence us, we are not determined by them. This, of course, is very much in line with the assumption that our actions, thoughts, and emotions are the product of our choices. Therefore, the key to changing any negative behavior lies in choosing to change what we do and think. We cannot change one without changing the other. Consequently, physiological *and* emotional change are inseparable as far as a successful process is concerned.

Existential-realism, the formulation combining existential and reality therapy, can achieve success by bringing about a positive and continuous "altered state" of understanding which will put into practice the precepts of personal responsibility. The primary focus is on the very nature of consciousness of the human condition, which certainly must include the capacity for self-awareness, freedom of choice to decide one's fate, responsibility, and an appreciation of our finiteness and ultimate death. This "state of mind" can help people become more effective in meeting their needs by challenging them to evaluate what they are doing — how they are living their lives — and to assess how well this behavior is working for them.

Along with the combining of the major tenets of existentialism and reality therapy, there is a third important ingredient which must be added to make the final formulation of existential-realism. Brief solution-oriented assumptions run throughout the therapeutic process, culminating in the completed recipe. Some of these assumptions are: Social reality is co-created. Resistance is not a useful concept. Small change is all that is necessary. Patients have resources to solve problems. Meanings are negotiable; choose meanings that lead to change. Rapid resolution of complaints is probable.

Child Development

A primary key to changing negative states of consciousness into positive states of consciousness, whether on an individual basis or a societal one, is the human foundation upon which one has to work and build. Because of massive amounts of erroneous information, received mostly through television, and then through "circular causality," which engulfs the general population on a daily basis, we have lost sight of the most workable and productive methods by which to raise our children. When we fail to be successful at that basic level, then we fail altogether.

As stated in other parts of this text, "circular causality" in this sense means simply that when a wrong thing is done, the media pick up on it, aggrandizes the wrong, makes it worse, then broadcasts it back out to the general public. It is then picked up by members of whatever profession it is aimed at, who utilize this wrong thing again within their particular field, at which point it is fed upon again by the media and the cycle continues over and over, growing more wrong and more harmful all the time.

In the developmental process, behavior is the product of learning. Children are both the products and the producers of their environment. Positive behavior is learned through reinforcement and imitation. Negative behavior is the result of faulty teaching. It is always good to remember that children will not pay attention to adults who act as if their foremost obligation is to pay attention to those children. Unless children pay more attention to you than you pay to them you cannot be either an effective role model or an effective teacher.

I live and work in San Antonio, Texas. It is a beautiful, friendly town with a population of about one million people. The following are examples of faulty teaching of our children today, taken out of local newspaper stories over just a few days (*San Antonio Express News*, August 11–17, 1994):

1. A national survey shows that young people are less honest today than ever before: 21 percent of all people under the age of 30 would cheat on just about anything if they could receive monetary gain from their dishonesty.
2. A 14-year-old boy kills his friend with an ice pick.
3. A 13-year-old girl stabs her teacher to death after an argument.
4. Students who fail their classes during the regular year are paid $600 apiece to attend summer school.
5. In a recent poll, 91 percent of six-year-old children showed

the same recognition factor for "Joe Cool," the Camel cigarette character, as for Mickey Mouse.

6. Cigarette smoking is on the decline among all age groups in America except teenagers. It is actually on the increase among those 18 years old and younger.

7. A Gallup poll showed that 62 percent of Americans believe the country is in moral decline. This is an increase of more than 20 percent from just ten years ago.

8. A high school honors student killed his parents and his two sisters, then calmly went on to school and told his teacher he was having a bad day.

9. When asked, Americans say they do not like violent shows on television. But violent shows, taken as a group, are always the most highly rated of all television programs.

10. Twenty percent of all murderers are 16 years old or younger.

11. The city of Fort Worth hires gang members and criminals to counsel other youngsters about the pitfalls of life.

12. More people than ever before believe they have been abducted by aliens.

13. More children are going to psychotherapists now than ever before in history.

14. Fewer people are willing to take responsibility for their lives now than ever before.

15. A local reporter was sympathetically asking a 14-year-old boy what he thought about the possibility of paddling being introduced at his junior high school. While the reporter was busy recording the boy's response, his friends stole her purse.

There are three basic, universal goals of parenting. In hierarchical order of importance the following are what parents should be most concerned about: (1) The basic physical survival and health of the child; (2) the proper development of the child's capacity to take care of him or herself in adulthood; (3) the development of the child's abilities for becoming a good, moral, contributing member of society. The reasons for the order are, of course, that you have to survive before anything else can happen, then you have to be able to care for yourself before you can worry about your image in the world or your potential contributions.

There are also, basically, three different approaches to parenting (Baumrind, 1975). There is the *authoritarian* approach. These parents are strict in the old-fashioned sense. They tell their children what is not allowed and that is the end of it, no argument. Hard work and respect are what they most wish to cultivate in their children. Then there is the *authoritative* approach. These parents are still quite firm, but they will explain the reasons for certain rules and regulations and they will allow some discussion. Third is the *permissive* approach. These parents adopt a "laissez-faire," or hands-off, attitude. They do not demand much from their children. They do tend to be helpful and generous, but they do not get a great deal in return.

As far as social development is concerned, children of authoritative parents tend to turn out best suited to carrying on a productive adult life. They adapt better to the stumbling blocks of life, they integrate socially with considerable ease, and they are quite aware of the fact that they are not the center of the universe. Children of authoritarian parents tend to lack independence and be somewhat hostile, and children of permissive parents tend to turn out worst of all: they display little self-control, have few friends, and remain rather immature.

Let us look at a number of possibilities in the area of the instructive upbringing with children. *Positive reinforcement* is the doing of something that will increase the likelihood of a desired response. An example would be to say, "Good job, way to go, I'm proud of you, son." *Negative reinforcement* is also applied in order to get a response, but the action on the parent's part is basically aimed at stopping something: "I'll stop yelling at you if you stop being disrespectful." *Positive punishment* is the doing of something rather than the undoing of something in order to get a response, "I will stop spanking you when you stop crying." *Negative punishment* is basically taking something away in order to stop a particular action: "You can't wear your favorite shirt to school until your grades get better."

It is always well to remember that particular punishments are judged by their effects and not their intentions. For example, parents, teachers, and even peers may use frowns and many other forms of verbal and nonverbal disapproval to discourage a child from performing an unwanted action. Nevertheless, attention, even when it is tinged with criticism or even mild corporal punishment, often serves as a "positive reinforcer." It increases the very behavior it is designed to discourage. Punishments ranging all the way from spankings to time-out techniques have been shown to be clearly effective, but only when the loss to the individual being punished is substantial enough to outweigh the reinforcers associated with the actions to be eliminated. And, very important, a parent, teacher, or other adult guardian should never reward a child for acting in an unacceptable fashion. For example, a child screams and throws a fit in a grocery store because he or she wants a piece of candy. The parent who then gives the child a piece of candy is teaching the child to scream and throw fits.

Interactions between the timing and intensity of punishments are very important. If a child does something you do not want him or her to do, punishment should be forthcoming right away. Higher-intensity punishment tends to cause a greater inhibition against repeating the act, but low-intensity also works if done quickly. High-intensity works even when delayed. Reasoning, along with either high- or low-intensity punishment, works better than not explaining why one is being punished. Basically, if your child does something you have said not to do, you have the responsibility as a proper parent to quickly follow through with an appropriate punishment which is severe enough to outweigh any reward the child may have received from the disobedient action. Telling a child that a particular punishment will follow an unwanted action and then not following through the very first time that unwanted action occurs is a strong sign of a deficit in parenting skills.

Certain precepts have been developed through many years of observation and study that indicate what most strongly contributes to the successful raising of children. In virtually every situation, if you reach out a helping hand to children, they will reach back. Children who are loved will give love in return. Children want and need guidance and discipline; you do no child a favor by being permissive and uninvolved. A parent who says something like "I love my child too much to punish her" really means that he or she does not love the child enough, or "loves" him or herself too much to take the time and energy it takes to raise a child in the best interest of the child.

The term "strong-willed child" implies that disobedience is a matter of some inherent temperamental trait. Disobedience is always a matter of parents and teachers who fail to communicate that they know where they stand, and know as well where they want the child to stand. Teaching proper behavior patterns is basically the same for all children. Adhering to good self-control makes for a stronger and longer lasting society, and the basis of such control breaks down into two distinct areas: resistance to temptation and delay of gratification. Children do not know what is in their own best interest. If they did, there would be absolutely no need for parents or teachers.

The therapeutic and developmental concepts discussed in this chapter are, of course, not new. However, bringing them all together into what I have termed "existential-realism" has some newness about it. More important, a great deal of the empirical data cited here indicates that the practical application of this combined process may increase the potential for "positive altered states" of consciousness, not only in counseling psychology but in society as a whole.

CHAPTER 8

Conclusions

Perception

Within all the topics and subtopics I have discussed under the main heading of "consciousness," there is a key element which intersects the entire compendium. That key element is *perception*. Whether one is speaking of overall consciousness, or its beginnings, or the biology of the brain from which consciousness arises, or science, pseudoscience, different methods of inquiry, linquistics, knowledge, awareness, hypnosis, victimization, existentialism, or what is "real," the mental process which is being most utilized is perception, both self-perception and social perception.

William James (1890) distinguished between the "me" (the self as an object of experience) and the "I" (the self as an active agent in the environment). James's concept of the "me" contains three distinct entities: the spiritual self, which is the inner core of identity, including one's goals, ambitions, and beliefs; the material self, which is one's physical attributes; and the social self, which is one's personal identity as it is known by others. According to James, the self extends beyond the physical body and includes a person's possessions, reputation, and family and social ties. A change in any of these changes a person's self-perception. These changes, of course, relate specifically to what has happened, or is happening to a person, good or bad, positive or negative.

Most, if not all, people tend to think of themselves as singular entities. However, we all contain a number of "selves." There is the self that attends classes, the one that communicates with his or her family, the one who is good or bad, and the one who is either "lucky" or "put upon" by one or more other persons. The self we present to the outside world continually changes, depending on who inhabits that world with us. How we see ourselves is almost never how others see us. This obviously can lead to much misunderstanding, misdirection, and miscommunication, all of which add up to erroneous perceptions. What people *think* happened, often did not happen at all. In reference to "incorrect" states of consciousness, the theory of self-perception (Bem, 1972) explains that people learn about their own attitudes, emotions, and other inner states by inferring them from their own and other people's behavior. We do not really have any advantage over an outsider when it comes to truly understanding what we feel or what we believe. We use the same external cues to define ourselves as other people do to define us.

The so-called Cartoon Experiment (Bem, 1965) illustrates Bem's theory of self-perception. Subjects were taught to use a colored light as a cue to accuracy. They were told to tell the truth in answering questions about themselves when the light was amber, and to lie when it turned green. Through this process, they learned to believe themselves when the light was amber but not to accept their own answers when the light was green. Later, when asked to decide whether magazine cartoons were "funny" or "unfunny," their opinions were found to be influenced by whether the "truth" light (amber) or the "lying" light (green) was on at the time. Their "real" attitudes about the cartoons varied according to the cues provided by the light; in other words, they perceived their own behavior in accord with outside dictates. This is exactly what can and often does happen in counseling and psychotherapy.

Much early research has been devoted to distinguishing between self-perception theory and dissonance theory. "Dissonance" refers to the psychological discomfort that occurs when two related conditions are in conflict. There is a normal human tendency to reduce this dissonance by altering one of the two conflicting conditions. A major question is, when do we engage in self-perception and when do we experience dissonance? Studies indicate that when behavior is congruent with one's attitudes, it is more appropriately explained by self-perception theory than by dissonance theory. On the other hand, when people are trying to understand something they have done that is in conflict with their attitudes, dissonance theory helps explain their behavior more appropriately (Fazio, Zanna, and Cooper, 1979). This also, of course, helps explain and feeds into the probability of manipulation, or influence, for good or bad within the therapeutic arena. "Influence" is a kinder word than "manipulation," but their meanings are basically the same. If I wanted to be aesthetically congruent, I could say that "influence" is used in therapy in accordance with the tenets of existential-realism, and that "manipulation" is used to spur "recovered memory" in many of the "general" counseling techniques which *search* for problems.

Although the issue of our awareness (consciousness) of our own mental processes is an old one in philosophy, it has only recently, as I stated earlier, gained the attention of a broad base of social scientists studying the human animal. And it has never, to my knowledge after intense research, been specifically investigated in reference to its relationship with the topics brought forth in this book. Social psychologists have long asked people to give their opinions on a particular topic (nuclear power, sex, their neighbors, etc.) or to explain why they engage in a particular behavior. But indications brought to light here, as well as elsewhere, are beginning to show that people cannot really provide accurate answers to such personal, "inner" questions. As I explained at some length earlier, people do not necessarily have direct access to their higher-order mental states, and therefore cannot give accurate accounts of the more complex aspects of their thinking.

Perception may actually be regarded as *the* fundamental aspect of consciousness. Overall, in many areas this process is obviously and rightfully referred to as "sensory" perception, which includes both exteroception and interoception. "Exteroception" pertains to the perception of external objects and events by means of our senses of vision, hearing, touch, taste, and smell. "Interoception" refers to the perception of body states and events, such as kinesthesis (sense of movement), proprioception (sense of body and limb position), and feelings of pain, internal pressure, stomach rumblings, and other discomforts.

Sensory perception ordinarily has priority in waking consciousness, because it is critical for guiding our interactions with the environment. Sensory perception is also the foundation, the starting place, of mental development. In the course of human growth, sensory perception develops first and then leads to higher levels of thinking, including imagery and conceptual thought. From this we can go to the constructivist theory explained earlier. The constructivist concept of perception says that everything of which we are "aware" is an interpretation of sensory data, based on our prior knowledge, beliefs, and expectations (Best, 1989). Usually, this process produces accurate, efficient schemata of the external world, but often, as our research has noted, errors or illusions can be the result — and more frequently now than ever before in human history. Again, perception is always the primary formulator of what goes into and what comes out of everything that entails the process of thought.

Summation

At the beginning of this book, we discussed methods of inquiry. Developments in the philosophy of science during the past few years have begun to produce major cracks in the consensus which was achieved during the previous half century around the theory of positivism. According to this mode of operation, scientific methods had to produce absolutely certain knowledge. Research results were judged according to a binary logic: knowledge was either true or it was not true. In relation to the study of human innuendo, allusion, feelings, emotions, and overall consciousness, it is now being more clearly understood that some claims about knowledge are better than others. Scientifically and pragmatically, this is a more common-sense understanding of knowledge. One can have more confidence in some scientific claims than in others without making a final choice between what is true (real) and what is not true (unreal).

In the chapter on the brain, the attempt was made to give basic overview of the incomparable wonder of this human organ. So much about the actions and interactions of its many billions of neurons, which transmit information in the form of electrochemical impulses, is so little understood. We know that impulses travel along neuron fibers called axons, which link regions of the central nervous system, the peripheral nervous system, and literally every other part of the human body. We know the "mechanics" of the engine, so to speak. But we know almost nothing about the product of the brain referred to as the "mind," or consciousness, or a combination of both. This, of course, is the very essence of "being." Everything else is just clothing.

We have a great many internal states and processes. We also have specific and innate mechanisms for differentiating the occurrence of some of these states and process from their nonoccurrence, as well as discriminating between them. When we invoke and attend to this kind of discriminatory activity, we then can make appropriate judgements about those internal states and processes, as framed in familiar perceptions (concepts) using common sense: "I feel happy,"

"I feel pain," "I see (have a sensation of) blue," and so forth. Therefore, spreading out those kinds of understandings (knowledge) to encompass everything possible in that line of thinking, we do have
some access to our own internal workings. Still, this access is woe-
fully incomplete. After all, *the mind is attempting to understand itself!* Astonishingly, headway is being made.

The crux of all the investigations, research, practical applications, and experiential and personal inquiries put forth in this book
is the attempt to understand *how* humans are enforced and reinforced in viewing their internal and external world. In order to obtain better and new information within that specific arena, we must
begin by understanding consciousness, to at least some extent, and
its relation to perceived reality. However, we must first determine
an appropriate *method*. We did, and explained why. We began,
logically, with a layperson's understanding of the brain before proceeding to lay out the multiplicities of consciousness. Only at that
point was it sensible to make a diligent, in-depth study of the great
many therapeutic approaches that seek to encourage — or coerce —
people, through mostly unknown mechanisms of the mind, into add-
ing a great negative *or* positive force into their lives.

Much of this book has been devoted to discussions and investigations in how to pragmatically define consciousness, particularly
in relation to the therapeutic process; the many difficulties that lie
in the path of reaching such a definition; and the most proper and
logical method for proceeding with the scientific inquiry into the
formulations and uses of understanding such a topic. Also shown, in
some detail, were several positive as well as negative results of altered states of consciousness, together with considerable additional
information which may add to further insights within the fields of
psychology and psychotherapy.

Topics for Investigation

A number of areas of human study may be enhanced by this book's
inquiries and by much further research within the field of the "management" of consciousness. Sleep and dream investigation, as well
as additional inquiry within the arenas of psychosis, meditation, and
biofeedback, may bring new tools to the problems of understanding
the many mysteries of the human species. And even further inquiry

into the extremely manipulative areas of hypnosis, suggestion, perception, and imagery cannot help but lead to the betterment of human personal development as well as more civilized, less violent social interactions.

Many types of psychotherapies address such areas as the client's feelings, unconscious memories, and multiple images. Worthwhile additions to empirical and theoretical pragmatism certainly could and would help to expand the concept of human beings and contribute to the possible discovery of new capacities of the species. Also, more holistic mental health systems are showing a considerable evolutionary trend toward involving the client more in her or his own treatment. Contemporary clinical implications of self-regulation, biofeedback, and self-hypnosis are solid examples of a trend toward more "intra" involvement.

Advances in the study of fantasy, imagination, and daydreaming continue to have notable implications for therapy. The role of imagination in therapeutic approaches to pain and disease management has already been well documented (Rossi, 1990). The profound changes in mental and physical responses that often accompany shifts from one altered state of consciousness to another provide additional evidence of the now obviously close connection between "mind," "consciousness," and "body."

It is quite clear now that consciousness, supported by all the research pertaining to this "mental introspection," is finally beginning to merge with the more traditional methods of therapy and transpersonal investigation. Some examples already given relate to such areas as the "present-centeredness" of existentialism, both as philosophy and psychotherapy, and the ever-continuing goal of obtaining a synthesis of the therapeutic process in order to gain a more holistic path to wellness.

Understanding of consciousness will continue to enhance the cognitive restructuring of personality by inducing a complementary relationship between intuition and intellect. Consequently, it is more apparent than ever that an ongoing, evolving partnership between the theoretical fields of consciousness research and the more clinical fields of counseling and psychotherapy will manifest itself in very significant ways in the not too distant future. My concept of existential-realism may be an example of that.

Our inquiry into the relationship of consciousness to the specific areas of methods of inquiry, the brain, "recovered" memory, and psychotherapy shows only too clearly that the considerable amount of research now taking place in the field of human awareness is extremely warranted. We are still some distance away from having a decent grasp of these matters. However, we know a good deal more than we did even ten years ago. The potential of what we might begin to know during the next ten, twenty, or thirty years is quite exciting indeed.

Societal Implications

The implications and usefulness of understanding and being aware of some of the major causes of these negative and positive altered states of consciousness are as important as they are all-encompassing. Again, therapy is manipulating or influential, depending on how one wishes to phrase it. The oppressive, directive therapy which searches for dysfunction will find it, even if it has to be made up from something as suspect as "recovered" memory. From that base one can make an extended, but totally valid, case for much of the reasoning behind the current negative state of our society as a whole.

Drawing on the conclusions of the data we have cited, let us see if we can formulate an educated supposition as to why our civilization seems to be imploding upon itself. As already shown in multiple studies, the majority of humans tend to behave as they believe they are "supposed" to behave. Where do virtually all of us learn our "lessons" on how to behave? There is absolutely no question about it: we get them from radio, television, motion pictures, and newspapers. The media teach us dysfunction in every possible form imaginable. Any sampling from any week in the mass media easily indicates that we are taught that "normal" people do not take responsibility for their own lives, "normal" people are born victims, and "normal" people whine and complain incessantly.

The fact of the matter is that, just as "recovered memory" patients have been taught a myth, inadvertently or not, by their psychotherapists, society as a whole is being taught a myth, inadvertently or not, by the mass media. What we are taught is *true* is not true; what we are taught is *normal* is not normal; what we are taught is *real* is not real. Nevertheless, by manipulation on a grand scale, human consciousness is coerced into *perceiving* fable as fact.

A high rating for a show on television, which reaches more people than all other types of media, would be around 15 points. In numbers of actual households watching, that can be rounded off to 15 million. Therefore, one could say that those people who continue to watch what they are being "taught" must be in at least some agreement with the content of the "lessons." Even that, of course, is a stretch in logic. Nevertheless, even if that stretch is accepted, it still falls miserably short of "normal." There are approximately 100 million households in the United States. Consequently, a very high-rated television show still draws only between 15 and 18 percent of the potential viewing audience. That means more than 80 percent are not watching it. However, the damage lies in the fact that we perceive that the actions depicted in the media are the norm. So, slowly but quite surely, we in society begin behaving that way—not taking responsibility, seeing ourselves as victims, whining, complaining, killing, and so forth. In a comparatively short period of time it can actually become the norm.

Kathleen Hall Jamieson, dean of the Annenberg School for Communication at the University of Pennsylvania, stated recently that the standards and patterns for all the media are being lowered to the shoddiest journalistic credentials possibly ever known in the history of the craft. A great percentage of "infotainment" programs have no credentials at all. However, this is where the majority of the populous becomes "informed" about anything and everything (Broder, 1994).

Just a passing glance at television and newspapers over an average few days (in February and March, 1994) tells the story. The Public Broadcasting Service announces a new series that will "explore the debate between creationism and Darwin's evolutionary theory" (Gunther, 1994). There is no "debate" possible. Creationism is fiction—pseudoscience. It is a religious myth and should not be given the same status as conclusions derived from scientific methods. NBC television viewers are subjected to a word-by-word interview with Jeffrey Dahmer, in which he describes his murder and dismemberment of more than 20 other humans (*Dateline*, NBC News, March 8, 1994). What positive usefulness can result from such an exhibition? A doctor's wife in Brownsville, Texas, is sentenced to life in prison for shooting a 17-year-old boy to death because he did not want to go steady with her daughter (*San Antonio Express News*, March 10, 1994, p. 11). A 22-year-old former beauty queen tries to kill an entire family by burning them to death because a female member of that family was dating a former boyfriend of hers (*Houston Chronicle*, March 3, 1994, p. 22). ABC news anchor Diane Sawyer eagerly coaxes every descriptive adjective out of convicted mass murderer Charles Manson as he describes, for the umpteenth time, his path of carnage 25 years ago. When asked if he is crazy, Manson gets off the most contemporarily relevant line heard in quite a while: "Sure I'm crazy, mad as a hatter, what difference does it make? You know, a long time ago, being crazy meant something. Nowadays, everybody's crazy" (Williams, 1994).

There seems to be a great difference of opinion about the extent to which the mass media, in particular television, influence the general populace. In actual fact, among the great majority of persons who study the subject there has long been virtually no difference of opinion at all. Of course the media have a strong influence on people from every facet of life. If they did not, businesses would not spend billions of dollars each year on advertising. Let us look at some of the latest research on the topic.

Envy can cause destructive impulses toward those persons who are perceived to have "good" things that the envier does not have. The impulses are aimed at destroying the desirable qualities shown by the envied person. The media continually put forth idealized people and lifestyles (Kreeger, 1992). Alcohol and cigarette companies target their advertising in the media much more heavily toward the black population than any other ethnic group in America (Altman, Schooler, and Basil, 1991). Habitual television viewers perceive that racial integration is more prevalent than it actually is (Matabane, 1988). The viewing of media violence is correlated with aggressive behavior (Huesmann, Eron, Berkowitz, and Chaffee, 1992). People can become "TV-dependent," and those persons that do, show a need to buy what they see on television and to believe what they see on television (Grant, Guthrie, and Ball-Rokeach, 1991). The media present a distorted view of law, crime, and justice (Hans and Dee, 1991). The media influence viewers in a negative manner. However, it is possible to use the media for positive manipulation (Wartella and Middlestadt, 1991). Corporate advertising in America has been successful in promoting positive images, services, products, and company position statements to a variety of audiences through extensive use of the mass media (Schumann, Hathcote, and West, 1991). And in the years following the electronic explosion which began shortly after World War II, the mass media have changed forever the elemental structure of modern American life, including politics, the electoral system, orthodox religion and church membership, entertainment, and the total concept of childhood (Friedlander, 1993). And, of course, this pervasive change in the foundational structure of what we view as "normal" is not limited to America. Looking in the direction of such countries as Bosnia-Herzegovina, Sudan, Somalia, Ethiopia, Rwanda, to name just a few, we see the violence and desolation that has led to the unnatural and heinous deaths of millions of our fellow human beings. These upheavals, bellowing within the fabric of civilization, should warn anyone who is even slightly paying attention that the animal known as *Homo sapiens* may, in fact, be on the brink of a new order of "reality" and consequently a seminal change in consciousness.

On the other side of the "influence" coin, if we use our potential altered states of consciousness for achieving with the help of counselors, psychotherapists, and even the mass media, in keeping with the principles of, for example, existential-realism, then it stands to reason that our present search for *problems* will be replaced, in the new conscious state, by a search for *solutions*. It is pervasive enough throughout history to be "common knowledge" that the great *bad* that some humans are capable of is equaled only by the great *good* that some humans are capable of. If our consciousness can be externally and massively influenced toward positive construction rather than negative destruction, as the situation is now, then, as a species, we may surely travel ever so much faster up the evolutionary ladder.

> Man is nothing but what he makes of himself. . . . Man first of all is the being who hurls himself toward a future and who is conscious of imagining himself as being in the future. Man is at the start of a plan which is aware of itself, rather than a patch of moss, a piece of garbage, or a cauliflower; nothing exists prior to this plan; there is nothing in heaven; man will be what he will have planned to be [Sartre, 1947, pp. 18–19].

References

Abel, G. G., Barlow, D. H., Blanchard, E., and Gould, D. (1977). The components of rapists' sexual arousal. *Archives of General Psychiatry, 34,* 395–403.

Ackerman, Norman J. (1984). *A theory of family systems* (pp. 177–215). New York: Gardner Press.

Ackerman, S. (1992). *Discovering the brain.* Washington, D.C.: National Academy Press.

Adelman, G. (Ed.). (1987). *Encyclopedia of neuroscience* (Vols. 1 and 2). Boston: Birkhauser.

Allport, F. H. (1924). *Social psychology.* Cambridge, MA: Riverside Press.

Allport, G. (1961). *Pattern and growth in personality.* New York: Holt, Rinehart & Winston.

Altman, D. G., Schooler, C., and Basil, M. D. (1991). Alcohol and cigarette advertising on billboards. *Health Education Research, 6(4),* 487–490.

Arbuckle, D. (1975). *Counseling and psychotherapy* (3rd ed., pp. 341–396). Boston: Allyn & Bacon.

Aron, M. (1982). *Hermeneutics of a complementarity between energy and meaning in Freud and implications for psychology.* Paper presented at the meeting of the Southeastern Psychology Association, New Orleans.

Aserinsky, E., and Kleitman, N. (1953). Regularly occurring periods of eye motility and concurrent phenomena during sleep. *Science, 118,* 114–122.

Asimov, I. (1987). *Beginnings: The story of organs — of mankind, life, the earth, the universe.* New York: Berkeley Books.

Associated Press compilation. (1990, May 14). *San Antonio Express News,* 4b.

Associated Press compilation. (1990, June 10). *San Antonio Express News,* 3E.

Associated Press compilation. (1993, November). *Los Angeles Times,* A12–13.

Associated Press Service. (1990, July).

Bandura, A. (1976). Conversation with Richard I. Evans. In R. E. Evans (Ed.), *The making of psychology.* New York: Knopf.

Bar-Tal, D. (1981). Motives for helping behavior expressed by kindergarten and school children in kibbutz and city. *Developmental Psychology, 17,* 776–792.

Baron, R. A. (1977). *Human aggression.* New York: Plenum.

Barrell, J. (1985, May). Human science research methods, understanding the structure of human experience. *West Georgia College Review, 16,* 35–38.

Baruss, I. (1986-87). Metanalysis of definitions of consciousness. *Imagination, Cognition, and Personality, 6,* 321–329.

Baumrind, D. (1975). *Early socialization and the discipline controversy.* Morristown, NJ: General Learning Press.

Bell, J. E. (1975). *Family therapy*. New York: Aronson.

Bem, D. J. (1965). An experimental analysis of self-perception. *Journal of Experimental Social Psychology, 1*, 199–218.

Bem, D. J. (1972). Self-perception theory. In L. Berkowitz (Ed.), *Advances in experimental social psychology*. New York: Academic Press.

Berkowitz, L. (1984). Some effects of thoughts on anti- and prosocial influences of media events: A cognitive-neoassociation analysis. *Psychological Bulletin, 95*, 410–427.

Bernard, J. (1985). *The adult years*. Cleveland, OH: International University Consortium.

Betrole, J. (1989, August). An ideal island, *Scientific American*, 24–29.

Best, J. B. (1989). *Cognitive psychology* (2nd ed.). St. Paul, MN: West.

Bordens, K. S., and Abbott, B. B. (1991). *Research design and methods* (pp. 146–181). London: Mayfield Publishing.

Bornstein, R. F. (1978). The exposure effect. In D. Druckman and J. A. Swet (Eds.), *Enhancing human performance* (1988). Washington, D.C.: National Academy Press.

Borg, W. R., and Gall, M. D. (1989). *Educational Research* (5th ed.). New York: Longman.

Bowers, K. S. (1984). On being unconsciously influenced and informed. In K. S. Bowers and D. Meichenbaum (Eds.), *The unconscious reconsidered* (pp. 227–272). New York: Wiley.

Brenton, M. (1966). *The American male*. New York: Coward-McCann.

Broder, D. (1994, February 24). Responsible media tell correct side of stories. *San Antonio Express News*, p. 4B.

Brown, J. H. (1986). *Family therapy: Theory and practice* (pp. 49–81). Monterey, CA: Brooks/Cole Publishing.

Calhoun, J. B. (1962, November). Population density and social pathology. *Scientific American, 206*, 139–148.

Campbell, D. T. (1965). Ethnocentric and other altruistic motives. In D. Levine (Ed.), *Nebraska symposium on motivation* (pp. 114–179). Lincoln: University of Nebraska Press.

Carmichael, S., and Hamilton, C. (1967). *Black power: The politics of liberation in America*. New York: Random House.

Carrington, P. (1977). *Freedom in meditation*. Garden City, NY: Anchor Press.

Center, J. (1990). *The futurist*. Bethesda, MD: World Future Society.

Churchland, P. (1983). *Matter and consciousness* (pp. 23–43). London: MIT Press.

Cleaver, E. (1969). *Soul on ice*. New York: Ramparts Books.

Cohen, B., and Itzhak, S. (1984). Using reality therapy with adult offenders. *Journal of Offender Counseling, 8*, 25–29.

Coram, G. J. and Hafner, J. L. (1988, December). Early recollections and hypnosis. *Individual Psychology: Journal of Adlerian Theory, Research and Practice, 44(4)*, 472–480.

Corey, G. (1983). *Theory and practice of group counseling*. Pacific Grove, CA: Brooks/Cole Publishing.

Corey, G. (1991). *Theory and practice of counseling and psychotherapy* (4th ed., pp. 171–199). Pacific Grove, CA: Brooks/Cole Publishing.

Corsini, R. J., and D. Wedding. (1989). *Current psychotherapies*. Itasca, IL: Peacock Publishers.

Crick, F., and Koch, C. (1992, September). The problems of consciousness. *Scientific American, 267,* 152–164.

Dallmayr, F. R., and McCarthy, T. A. (1977). *Understanding social inquiry.* Notre Dame, IN: University of Notre Dame Press.

Dillbeck, M. C., Banus, C. B., Polanzi, C., and Landrith, G. S. III. (1988). Test of a field model of consciousness and social change. *Journal of Mind and Behavior, 142,* 457–486.

Dobkin de Rios, M. (1984). *Hallucinogens: Cross-cultural perspectives.* Albuquerque: University of New Mexico Press.

Donnerstein, E. (1984). Pornography: Its effects on violence against women. In N. M. Malamuth and E. Donnerstein (Eds.), *Pornography and sexual aggression* (pp. 188–202), New York: Academic Press.

Efron, H. S. (1967). Meditation as an adjunct to psychotherapy. *New dimensions in psychiatry: A world view.* New York: Wiley Press.

Eliot, S., and Stern, B. (1979). *The age of enlightenment: An anthology of eighteenth-century texts* (Vol. 2). College Park, MD: Ward Lock Educational.

Evans, R. C. (1979). Dream conception and reality testing in children. *Journal of the American Academy of Child Psychiatry, 22,* 47–59.

Farber, I. E. (1963). The things people say to themselves. *American Psychologist, 18,* 185–197.

Farthing, G. W. (1992). *The psychology of consciousness* (pp. 64–88). Englewood Cliffs, NJ: Prentice-Hall.

Fazio, R. H., Zanna, M. P., and Cooper, J. (1979). Dissonance and self-perception: An integrative view of each theory's proper domain of application. *Journal of Experimental Social Psychology, 13,* 87–103.

Feis, C. L., Mavis, B. D., Weth, J. E., and Davidson, W. S. (1990). Graduate training and employment experiences of community psychologists. *Professional Psychology: Research and Practice, 21(4),* 95–98.

Feltz, D. L., and Landers, D. M. (1983). The effects of mental practice on motor skill learning and performance: A meta-analysis. *Journal of Sport Psychology, 5(1),* 25–57.

Ferenczi, S. (1926). An attempted explanation of some hysterical stigmata. In *Further contributions to the theory and technique of psychoanalysis.* London: Hogarth Press.

Fischer, R. (1986). Toward a neuroscience of self-experience and states of self-awareness and interpreting interpretations. In B. B. Wolman and M. Ullman (Eds.), *Handbook of states of consciousness* (pp. 1–26). New York: Van Nostrand Reinhold.

Flanagan, J. C. (1987). A research approach to improving our quality of life. *American Psychologist, 33,* 138–147.

Foreman, H. (1978). *Racism and inequality.* San Francisco: Freeman & Company.

Frankl, V. (1967). *Psychotherapy and existentialism* (pp. 87–95). New York: Washington Square Press.

Friedlander, B. Z. (1993). Community violence, children's development, and mass media: In pursuit of new insights, new goals, and new strategies. *Psychiatry: Interpersonal and biological processes, 56,* 10–35.

Furman, B., and Tapani, A. (1989). Adverse effects of psychotherapeutic beliefs. *Family Systems Medicine, 7(2),* 33–38.

Gill, M. M., and Brenman, M. (1959). *Hypnosis and related states.* (New York: International Universities Press.

Glasser, W. (1965). *Reality therapy.* New York: Harper & Row.

Glasser, W. (1969). *Schools without failure.* New York: Harper & Row.

Glasser, W. (1975). *Reality therapy* (3rd ed.). New York: Harper & Row.

Glasser, W. (1977). *The identity society.* New York: Harper & Row.

Goldenberg, I., and Goldenberg, H. (1985). *Family therapy.* Pacific Grove, CA: Brooks/Cole Publishing.

Goldstein, M., and Goldstein, I. E. (1978). *How we know.* New York: Da Capo Press.

Goleman, D. (1977). *The varieties of meditative experience.* New York: E. P. Dutton.

Grant, A. E., Guthrie, K. K., and Ball-Rokeach, S. J. (1991). Television shopping: A media system dependency perspective. *Communication Research, 18(6),* 773–798.

Gray, E. B., Lovejoy, M. C., Piotrkowski, C. S., and Bond, J. T. (1990). Husband supportiveness and the well-being of employed mothers of infants. *Families in Society: The Journal of Contemporary Human Services, 24,* 145–152.

Gunther, M. (1994, February 25). Funding decisions perceived as turn to right for public TV. *San Antonio Express News,* pp. 1H, 9H.

Gurman, A. S., and Raxin, A. M. (1987). *Effective psychotherapy.* New York: Pergamon Press.

Hales, S. (1986). Rethinking the business of psychology. *The Journal for the Theory of Social Behavior, 16,* 57–76.

Haley, J. (1980). *Problem-solving therapy.* San Francisco: Jossey-Bass.

Hans, V. P., and Dee, J. L. (1991). Media coverage of law: Its impact on juries and the public. *American Behavioral Scientist, 35(2),* 136–149.

Hempel, C. G. (1966). *Philosophy of natural science.* Englewood Cliffs, NJ: Prentice-Hall.

Hoffman, L. (1988). A constructivist position for family therapy. *The Irish Journal of Psychology, 9,* 110–129.

Huesmann, L. R., Eron, L. D., Berkowitz, L., and Chaffee, S. (1992). The effects of television violence on aggression: A reply to a skeptic. *Psychology and Social Policy, 79,* 191–200.

Irwin, H. J. (1989). *An introduction to parapsychology.* Jefferson, NC: McFarland & Co.

Irwin, H. J. (1992). Origins and functions of paranormal belief: The role of childhood trauma and interpersonal control. *Journal of the American Society for Psychical Research, 86(3),* 249–256.

Is sex abuse on the rise? (1993, September). *Los Angeles Times,* p. D2.

James, W. (1890). *The principles of psychology.* New York: Henry Holt & Co.

Jensen, J. P., Bergin, A. E., and Greaves, D. W. (1990). The meaning of eclecticism: New survey and analysis of components. *Professional Psychology: Research and Practice, 21(6),* 124–130.

June, L., and Curry, B. (1990). An 11-year analysis of black students' experience of problems and use of services: Implications for counseling professionals. *Journal of Counseling Psychology, 37,* 48–66.

Kamiya, J. (1971). *Conditioned discrimination of the EEG alpha rhythm in humans: Biofeedback and self-control.* Chicago: Aldine/Atherton.

Kanter, R. M. (1985). *Jobs and families: Impact of working roles on family life.* Cleveland, Ohio: International University Consortium.

Karl, R. and Hamalian, L. (Eds.). (1963). *The existential imagination.* New York: Fawcett Publications.

Kelly, E. F. and Locke, R. G. (1981). *Altered states of consciousness and psi: An historical survey and research prospects.* New York: Parapsychological Foundation.

King, M.L., III. (1990, January). The equality of finances, *Omni,* 30–36.

Keynes, M. (1986). *The French enlightenment.* London: Open University Press.

Kline, M. V. (1958). *Freud and hypnosis: The interaction of psychodynamics and hypnosis.* New York: Julian Press.

Knowles, E. S. (1973). Boundaries around group interaction: The effect of groups size and member status on boundary permeability. *Journal of Personality and Social Psychology, 26,* 327–331.

Kreeger, L. (1992). Envy preemption in small and large groups. *Group Analysis, 25(4),* 391–408.

Krippner, S. (Ed.) (1990). *Dreamtime and dreamwork.* Los Angeles: Tarcher.

Krippner, S. and Dillard, J. (1988). *Dreamworking.* Buffalo, NY: Bearly.

Krippner, S., and Maliszewski, M. (1978). Meditation and the creative process. *Journal of Indian Psychology, 1,* 40–58.

Kuhn, T. (1963). The function of dogma in scientific research. In *Scientific knowledge: Basic issues in the philosophy of science* (pp. 253–265). Chicago: University of Chicago Press.

L'Abate, L., Ganahl, G., and Hansen, J. C. (1986). *Methods of family therapy.* Englewood Cliffs, NJ: Prentice-Hall.

Lask, B. (1989). Editorial—flying gurus and their recursive interactions. *Journal of Family Therapy, 11,* 315–318.

Lemann, N. (1986, July). Origins of the underclass. *The Atlantic Monthly, 258,* 31–61.

Lerner, M. J. (1970). Desire for justice and reactions to victims. In J. Macauley and L. Berkowitz (Eds.), *Altruism and helping behavior.* New York: Academic Press.

Lerner, M. J. (1980). *The belief in a just world: The fundamental delusion.* New York: Plenum.

Lerner, M. J. (1982). The justice motive in human relations and the economic model of man: A radical analysis of facts and fictions. In V. J. Derlega and J. Grzelak (Eds.), *Cooperation and helping behavior: Theories and research.* New York: Academic Press.

Lilly, J. C. (1982). *The human biocomputer.* New York: Julian Press.

Loftus, E. (1980, July). The incredible eyewitness. *Psychology Today, 7,* 117–119.

Logan, R. W. (1965). *The Negro in the United States.* Toronto: Nostrand Publishing.

Loury, G. (1990, February). Speech before the Heritage Foundation, Harvard University. (From viewing the speech on C-SPAN.)

Lum, D. (1986). *Social work practice and people of color: A process-stage approach.* Monterey, CA: Brooks-Cole.

Lycan, W. G. (1987). Toward a homuncular theory of believing. *Cognition and Brain Theory, 4,* 2.

Lynn, S. J., Milano, M., and Weekes, J. R. (1992). Pseudomemory and age regression: An exploratory study. *American Journal of Clinical Hypnosis, 35,* 129–137.

Macauley, J. R., and Berkowitz, L. (1970). *Altruism and helping behavior.* New York: Academic Press.

McGoldrick, M., Pearce, K., and Giordano, J. (1982). *Ethnicity and family therapy.* New York: Guilford Press.

McHugh, D. (1993, January 17). "Recovered" memory challenged. *San Antonio Express News,* p. D7.

McKim, W. A. (1986). *Drugs and behavior: An introduction to behavioral psychopharmacoloy.* Englewood Cliffs, NJ: Prentice Hall.

McNally, R. J., and Heatherton, T. F. (1993). Are covariation biases attributable to a priori expectance biases? *Behavior Research and Therapy, 31(7),* 653–658.

Marino, Thomas. O.J. aftermath. American Counseling Association (1993, Sept.) pp. 12–13, *The Guidepost.* L.A. Times Publishers.

Masden, J. (1984). *In search of consciousness.* New York: Trimark Press.

Maslow, A. J. (1962). *Toward a psychology of being.* New York: Van Nostrand.

Masson, J. M. (1988). *Against therapy: Emotional tyranny and the myth of psychological healing.* New York: Atheneum.

Matabane, P. W. (1988). Television and the black audience: Cultivating moderate perspectives on racial integration. *Journal of Communication, 38(4),* 21–31.

May, R. (1981) *Freedom and destiny.* New York: W. W. Norton & Co.

May, R. (1983). *The discovery of being.* New York: W. W. Norton & Co.

Medina, C. (1974). *Chicanos: Existentialism and the human condition.* Berkeley, CA: Marfel Associates.

Mencken, H. L. (1917, September 1). Fakes and frauds. *St. Louis Post Dispatch,* p. 37.

Michelozzi, B. N. (1988). *Coming alive from nine to five.* Mountain View, CA: Mayfield Publishing Co.

Mill, J. S. ([1848] 1899). *Principles of political economy* (Vol. 1). New York: Colonial Press.

Miller, N. E. (1992). Some examples of psycho-physiology and the unconscious. *Biofeedback and Self-Regulation, 17,* 3–16.

Mind and brain. (1992, September). *Scientific American* [Special Issue].

Mingay, D. J. (1986). Hypnosis and memory for incidentally learned scenes. *British Journal of Experimental and Clinical Hypnosis, 3,* 173–183.

Minuchin, S. (1984). *Family kaleidoscope.* Cambridge, MA: Harvard University Press.

Morrissey, Mary (1993, Oct.). Terror in the hallways. American Counseling Association. *The Guidepost,* p. 6 and 20. L. A. Times Publishers.

Morrissey, Mary (1994, Jan.). Sexual harassment. American Counseling Association. *The Guidepost,* pp. 14–17. L. A. Times Publishers.

Mydell, M. (1990). Understanding Arabs. *Journal of Cross-Cultural Psychology, 21(1),* 35–46.

Nash, M. R. (1988). Hypnosis as a window on regression. *Bulletin of the Menninger Clinic, 52,* 383–403.

Natsoulas, T. (1978). Consciousness. *American Psychologist, 33,* 906–914.

Natsoulas, T. (1983). Addendum to "Consciousness." *American Psychologist, 38,* 121–125.

Natsoulas, T. (1988). The intentionality of retrowareness. *Journal of Mind and Behavior, 9,* 549–573.

O'Brian, C. (1990). Family therapy with black families. *Journal of Family Therapy, 12,* 18–22.

O'Hanlon, W., and Weiner-Davis, M. (1989). *In search of solutions*. New York: W. W. Norton & Co.

One woman in three said to be abused. (1994, March). *USA Today*, p. A3.

Orne, M. T. (1989). *Reconstructing memory through hypnosis: Forensic and clinical implications*. New York: Guilford Press.

Pascarella, P. (1984). *The new achievers*. New York: Free Press.

Pattison, E. M., and Kahan, J. (1986). Conceptual tool for modes of consciousness. In B. B. Wolman and M. Ullman (Eds.), *Handbook of states of consciousness* (pp. 199–248). New York: Van Nostrand Reinhold.

Pavlov, I. P. (1923). The identity of inhibition with sleep and hypnosis. *Scientific Monthly, 17*, 603–608.

Pedersen, P. (1990). *A Handbook for developing multicultural awareness*. London: New Day Publications.

Pekala, R. J., Kumar, V. K., and Cummings, J. (1992). Types of high hypnotically susceptible individuals and reported attitudes and experiences of the paranormal and the anomalous. *Journal of the American Society for Psychical Research, 86*, 135–150.

Penrod, S. (1986). *Social psychology* (pp. 209–226). Engelwood Cliffs, NJ: Prentice-Hall.

Pettigrew, T. (1975). *A profile of the Negro American*. Toronto: Nostrand.

Polkinghorne, D. (1983). *Methodology for the human science* (pp. 241–281). Albany: State University of New York Press.

"Prisoners of Silence." (1993, December). *Frontline*. New York: Public Broadcasting Service.

Purce, J. (1974). *The mystic spiral*. London: Thames & Hudson.

Putnam, W. H. (1979). Hypnosis and distortions in eyewitness memory. *International Journal of Clinical and Experimental Hypnosis, 27*, 437–448.

Radner, D., and Radner, M. (1982). *Science and unreason*. Belmont, CA: Wadsworth Publishing.

Recollections of sex abuse challenged. (1993, November 26). *San Antonio Express News*, p. 9C.

Researchers indicate some people spend half of their day in fantasy. (1987, April 3). *The New York Times*, sec. 7, p. 4.

Rosenthal, R. (1991). *The conscious brain*. New York: Vintage Books.

Rossi, E. L. (1990). From mind to molecule: More than a metaphor. In J. K. Zeig and S. Gilligan (Eds.), *Brief therapy* (pp. 445–472). New York: Brunner-Mazel.

Rubin, Z. (1974). From liking to loving: Patterns of attraction in dating relationships. In T. L. Huston (Ed.), *Foundations of interpersonal attraction*. New York: Academic Press.

Ruggiero, V. (1984). *The art of thinking*. New York: Bowden.

Sagan, C. (1980). *Cosmos*. New York: Random House.

Sahiro, J., and Budman, B. (1973). *Family strategy*. New York: Trimark Press.

Sammons, M. T., and Gravitz, M. A. (1990). Theoretical orientations of professional psychologists and their former professors. *Professional Psychology: Research and Practice, 21(10)*, 131–134.

San Antonio Express-News (1992, June 13, p. B3).

Saraceno, C. (1990). The concept of family strategy. *Marriage and Family Review, 14(1–2)*, 12–16.

Sarnoff, D. (1982). Biofeedback: New uses in counseling. *Personnel and Guidance Journal, 60,* 357–360.

Sartre, J. P., Frechtman, B. (Trans.). (1947). *Existentialism.* New York: Philosophical Library.

Sartre, J. P., Barnes, H. E. (Trans.). (1957). Existentialism and human emotions (pp. 11–35). New York: Wisdom Library.

Schneck, J. M. (1963). *Hypnosis in modern medicine.* Springfield, IL: Thomas.

Schumann, D. W., Hathcote, J. M., and West S. (1991). Corporate advertising in America: A review of published studies on use, measurement, and effectiveness. *Journal of Advertising, 20(3),* 35–56.

Seligson, M., Fersh, E., Marshall, N. L., and Marx, F. (1990). School-age child care: The challenge facing families. *Journal of Economic Issues, 24,* 145–152.

Shapiro, R. (1987). *Origins: A skeptic's guide to the creation of life on earth.* New York: Bantam Books.

Sheehan, P. W. (1988). Memory distortion in hypnosis. *International Journal of Clinical and Experimental Hypnosis, 36,* 296–311.

Sheehan, P. W., Garnett, M., and Robertson, R. (1993). The effects of cue level, hypnotizability, and state instruction on responses to leading questions. *International Journal of Clinical and Experimental Hypnosis, 41(4),* 287–304.

Sheehan, P. W., Green, V., and Truesdale, P. (1992). Influence of rapport on hypnotically induced pseudomemory. *Journal of Abnormal Psychology, 101,* 690–700.

Sheikh, A. A., and Shaffer, J. T. (Eds.). (1979). *The potential of fantasy and imagination.* New York: Brandon House.

Shepard, R. N., and Cooper, L. N. (1982). *Mental images and their transformations.* Cambridge, MA: MIT Press.

Sherif, M. (1936). *The psychology of social norms.* New York: Harper.

Siever, R. (1968, January). Science: Observational, experimental, historical. *Scientific American, 56,* 70–71.

Skinner, B. F. (1967). *The behavior of organisms.* New York: Appleton Century Crofts.

Skinner, B. F. (1973). *About behaviorism.* New York: Knopf.

Skinner, B. F. ([1971] 1980). *Beyond freedom and dignity.* New York: Bantam Books.

Skinner, B. F. (1983). *A matter of consequences.* New York: Knopf.

Skinner, B. F. (1987). *Upon further reflection.* Englewood Cliffs, NJ: Prentice-Hall.

Smith, D. (1982). Trends in counseling and psychotherapy. *American Psychologist, 37,* 802–809.

Snow, T. P. (1985). *The dynamic universe.* New York: West Publishing Co.

Spanos, N. P., and McLean, J. (1986). Hypnotically created pseudomemories: Memory distortions or reporting biases? *British Journal of Experimental and Clinical Hypnosis, 3(3),* 155–159.

Spanos, N. P., Lush, N. I., and Gwynne, M. I. (1989). Cognitive skill-training enhancement of hypnotizability: Generalization effects and trance logic responding. *Journal of Personality and Social Psychology, 56(5),* 795–804.

Springer, S. P., and Deutsch, G. (1989). *Left brain, right brain.* New York: W. H. Freeman & Company.

Stanton, J., and Todd, S. (1979). *Drug addiction therapy.* New York: Renn Co.

Steiner, I. D. (1972). *Group process and productivity.* New York: Academic Press.

Sundberg, N. (1973). *Clinical psychology: Expanding horizons*. New York: Appleton-Century.

Tajfel, H. (1982). Social psychology of intergroup relations. *Annual Review of Psychology, 33,* 1–39.

Tarcher, J. T. (1983). *The global brain*. Los Angeles: Steven & Company.

Taylor, C. ([1971] 1977). Interpretation and the sciences of man. In F. Dallmayr and T. McCarthy (Eds.). *Understanding and social inquiry*. London: University of Notre Dame Press.

Teplin, L. (1990). Detecting disorder: The treatment of mental illness among jail detainees. *Journal of Consulting and Clinical Psychology, 58(2),* 367–379.

Terkel, S. (1972). *Working*. New York: Random House.

Thomas, C. (1990, January 30). Discrimination by blacks. *The San Antonio Light*, p. B7.

Thompson, C., and Rudolph, L. (1988). *Counseling children*. Pacific Grove, CA: Brooks/Cole Publishing.

Toffler, A. (1980). *The third wave*. New York: William Morrow & Co.

Tonay, V. K. (1993). Personality correlates of dream recall: Who remembers? *Dreaming: Journal of the Association for the Study of Dreams, 3(1),* 1–8.

Underwood, B., and Moore, B. (1982). Perspective-taking and altruism. *Psychological Bulletin, 91,* 143–183.

United States Chamber of Commerce (compilation study). (1985). *Workers' attitudes toward productivity* (p. 11).

U. S. Government Printing Office, United States Labor Department. (1990). *Children at work* (p. 22).

Van Kaam, A. (1966). *The art of existential counseling*. Wilkes-Barre, PA: Dimension Books.

Wagstaff, G. F. (1981). *Hypnosis, compliance, and belief*. New York: St. Martin's Press.

Wartella, E., and Middlestadt, S. (1991). The evolution of models of mass communication and persuasion. *Health Communication, 3(4),* 205–215.

Watkins, C. E., Schneider, L. J., Manus, M., and Hunton-Shoup, J. (1990). Terminal master's level training in counseling psychology: Skills, competencies, and student interests. *Professional Psychology: Research and Practice, 21,* 216–218.

Watkins, J. G. and Watkins, H. H. (1986). States of consciousness in B. B. Wolman and M. Ullman (Eds.), *Hypnosis, multiple personality, and ego states as altered states of consciousness* (pp. 133–156, ch. 5). New York: Van Nostrand Reinhold.

Watson, J. B. (1967). *Behavior: An introduction to comparative psychology*. New York: Holt, Rinehart & Winston.

Werry, J. S. (1989). Family therapy—professional endeavour or successful religion? *Journal of Family Therapy, 2,* 377–382.

Whitaker, C. A. (1977). *Process techniques of family therapy*. New York: Blakiston.

Williams, J. B., and Spitzer, R. (1983). *Psychotherapy research*. New York: Guilford Press.

Williams, R. (1989). *Toward a self-managed life-style*. Boston: Houghton Mifflin.

Williams, S. (1994, March 9). Sawyer digs up Manson murders for premiere of "Turning Point." *San Antonio Express News*, p. 19H.

Wilson, E. O. (1975). *Sociobiology: The new synthesis.* Cambridge, MA: Harvard University Press.

Wonder, J., and Donovan, P. (1984). *Whole brain thinking* (pp. 147–211). New York: Ballantine Books.

Yalom, I. D. (1980). *Existential psychotherapy.* New York: Basic Books.

Yalom, I. D. (1989). *Love's executioner.* New York: Basic Books.

Yandel, K. (1977). *Philosophy and ethics.* Madison, WI: University of Wisconsin Press.

Zelig, M., and Beidleman, W. B. (1981). The investigative use of hypnosis: A word of caution. *International Journal of Clinical and Experimental Hypnosis, 29,* 401–412.

Index